Steven Fleming

# VELOTOPIA

## the production of cyclespace in our minds and our cities

nai010 publishers

# VELOTOPIA

**Proposition 1: New York**

**From a Pedestrian
to a Bike City**

**Proposition 2: Copenhagen**

**From a City for Horses
to a City for Cyclists**

**Proposition 3: Sydney**

**From a City for Driving
to a City for Cycling**

**Proposition 4: Newcastle**

**From Brownfields
to Bike Fields**

Before we discard our bodies to become spiritual machines
Before we replace our friends with synthesized substitutes
Before we eliminate our emotions in favour of perfect logic
Before we surrender our autonomy to smart objects, vehicles and cities

Let us pause

And examine a 200-year-old technology driving adoption rates
that would make any Silicon Valley investor drool. And let us do this
through the prism of Stanley Kubrik's masterpiece *2001: A Space Odyssey.*

In the climactic turning point, our human hero deactivates HAL- the Artificial
Intelligence meant to care for all life-support mechanisms of the spaceship.

This very act set the stage for humanity's next great evolution.

As HAL reaches the end-stage of synthetic life, his last words
are from his first implanted memory. A song called *Daisy Bell.*
A song about a boy who longs to be with his love on a bicycle.

'You'll look sweet upon the seat of a bicycle built for two'

Let us wonder:

Where can the bicycle take us?

Lee Feldman
CycleSpace, 2017

## A Mum With a Bub in a Box Bike

1
Lebbeus Woods,
'Anarchitecture:
Architecture is a Political
Act', in: *Lebbeus Woods,
Architectural Monograph
#22* (New York: Academy
Editions, 1993).

At the centre of this book is a protagonist, a hypothetical mother whose simple aims – health, safety, money and getting to places in the city she lives in – mean she is better off cycling to the shops than driving a car. Who is she exactly?

'Call this person the inhabitant. Call this person yourself.'[1] These are the words of Lebbeus Woods from an essay about architects' complicity with politicians and profit-obsessed clients who conform to the will of mass markets 'at the expense of some person who is not willing to do so. To construct a just society', Woods argues, 'it is precisely this lone person who must first receive justice.'

## Bicycle-Centric Urban Growth:
## Seeing beyond the Urban Renewal Agenda

Bicycle transport was redefined for the world in 2010. That was the year the world's bellwether city, New York, reallocated space for motorized transport to human-powered transport with its protected bike lanes. Now there is hardly a city in the developed world that isn't at least talking about becoming bike friendly. But let's not get too excited. Most cities have been talking about the needs of the blind and disabled.

Our thinking would be a lot clearer if we were up front about bicycling's worth. Sure, it can be a way of redeeming the suburbs, combatting global warming and improving public health. It can also be an end in itself.

But where it is getting the most love from politicians is in the gentrified inner city. As people move back to the city their old suburban habit of driving makes traffic grind to a halt. They realise cars in the city are like popcorn in a funnel. They start cycling, reading Jane Jacobs, visiting Copenhagen, lobbying for bicycle lines, reading Jan Gehl, hating on people driving in from the suburbs and thinking of themselves as 'bicycle urbanists'.

What the petite bourgeoisie are not asking is how cycling might influence urban growth, not just urban renewal. When we shift our focus from urban renewal and gentrification to urban growth, cycling becomes a big topic. It goes from being something North Americans might want for their gentrified hoods to something that can underpin rapidly growing cities, especially in the developing world. For those who would call themselves bicycle urbanists the focus would shift from trifling interventions like protected bike lanes and lower speed limits to grand visions of car-free cities, indoor cities, cities with buildings designed for riding inside, etcetera.

Two things make this unthinkable to the built environment designer community. First is a belief, ever since London's population grew to 6 million before the 'safety-bicycle' (two equal-sized wheels and a chain drive) was even invented, that the industrialized city cannot exist without industrial modes of transportation: the steam train, the street car, the driverless car or whatever. Second is the inordinate influence of consensus-view urban designers, in the ilk of Jane Jacobs and Jan Gehl. Now a whole generation can't see the difference between observing urban spaces that already exist and producing new urban space on brownfields and greenfields. There are 'urban designers' who do nothing but analyse data. Exactly how much are they waiting to gather before doing more with it than arranging moveable deck chairs on what might be a kind of Titanic?

It is not within the means of this planet to serve the bourgeoning cities of the world's poorer regions with motorized transportation. That leaves us with two options: planning cities where people stay put in their walkable sphere (how depressing!) or, seeing how far we can go with the idea of planning cities where everyone uses super-cheap means of connecting to markets, most obviously cycling. Quickly then, let's extricate the topic of bicycle urbanism from the topic of urban renewal. Let's see cycling occasioning a period of architectural inventiveness of Asian or South American proportions. That will mean swapping the empiricism of Jan Gehl and Jane Jacobs for the more daunting epistemology of someone like Le Corbusier.

What is so clever about Le Corbusier's buildings are their unbroken teleological connections to the realities of his time. One reality was the new plastic material, reinforced concrete, that could liberate wall planes from their former floor and roof bearing duties; Le Corbusier's Villa Savoye demonstrates the full ramifications.

In its siting, on the formerly unreachable outskirts of Paris, the Villa Savoye demonstrates the ramifications of two more realities of the interwar period: people's fear of infectious diseases in the wake of the 1918 influenza pandemic, and their enthusiasm for the fantastic machine that could separate every human one from the other: the car.

No one would say Le Corbusier's Plan Voisin did good for the world, but we can learn so much from his logical process. If Le Corbusier were alive now, grappling with the problems that face us (and if his sponsor wasn't the car maker Voisin but a bicycle brand), what new vision for cities would he devise?

# From a Pedestrian to a Bike City

# proposition 1

# New York

The Chelsea-Elliot houses in New York sacrifice density and street life for the idea that everyone in the city might own their own car.

The car-city paradigm was introduced to New Yorkers in an exhibition called Futurama at their 1939 World's Fair. The idea was to make buildings tall and thin so that down at ground level there would be space for much wider roads – mobility for mobility's sake.

1939 Futurama, Norman Bel Geddes, Library of Congress

Jane Jacobs, 1965. Credit: Bob Gomel/The LIFE Images Collection, via Getty Images

What they got were towers in a carpark where people felt frightened to walk.

Chelsea, New York, on Google Earth

Too few New Yorkers have the
luxury of walking to work.
Most have to use trains.

These blocks could be redeveloped in the manner of their pre-WW2 neighbours elsewhere in Chelsea, with walk-up flats and walkable streets.

But is that the best we can do?

More though are swapping walking and trains for another mode that can get them to work, school, shops … even the beach. It burns more fat and is good for the city.

Bicycle Commuting in Chelsea, New York City

In the spirit of
the Worlds' Fairs
let us imagine
New York as a
city where almost
everyone cycles.

Design gradients to suits riders who
need to carry children or goods.

A loaded cargo bike is brought to a stop by a two meter rise

## Use shops as columns

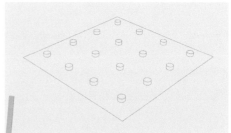

Use the shops to hold up the buildings so at ground level cyclists can go as the crow flies.

## Pedestrian city

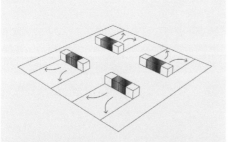

Originally conceived as a city for walking New York has a street grid that funnels people down a limited number of avenues where they can find all the shops, and the shops can find them. Take the shops that cyclists can't see as they are riding by quickly and use them to bring life to the side streets.

## Make mounds

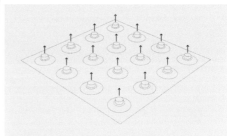

To save cyclists from having to brake to slow down, lift all the shops onto mounds.

## Move shops to side streets

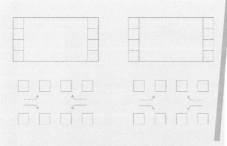

Let the gaps between shops be ground-level through-ways.

## Bridging fast zones

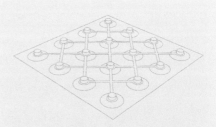

Separate strollers from rollers with an elevated network of bridges connecting the crests.

Canopies would give people on bikes the same protection from the sun and the rain as they would have if they were driving or going by train.

Low will mean go …

…and high will mean slow.

## Build aerial streets

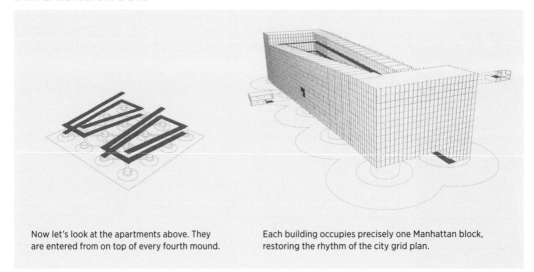

Now let's look at the apartments above. They are entered from on top of every fourth mound.

Each building occupies precisely one Manhattan block, restoring the rhythm of the city grid plan.

## Build spiraling streets

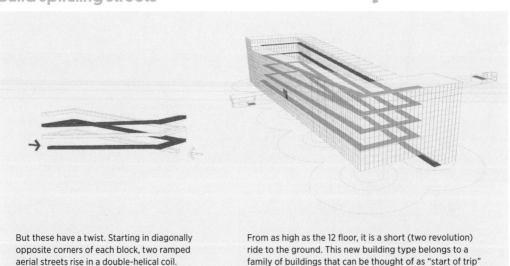

But these have a twist. Starting in diagonally opposite corners of each block, two ramped aerial streets rise in a double-helical coil.

From as high as the 12 floor, it is a short (two revolution) ride to the ground. This new building type belongs to a family of buildings that can be thought of as "start of trip" facilities for the future bike city.

## Make efficient use of wide aerial streets

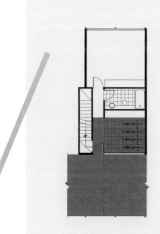
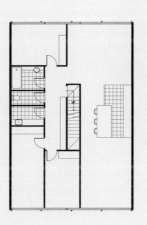

Using interlocking cross-over and cross-under apartments, it is possible to provide gallery access (here coloured blue) to one third of all levels, without compromising efficiency. Here is a large cross-under apartment.

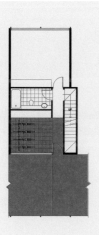
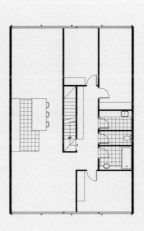
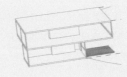

And here is its neighbour, a cross-over apartment. There would be a few single storey apartments in any block for the disabled. But as a society we are building too many of those, and not enough two-storey/dual-aspect apartments with better access to sun and cross-ventilation.

The site falls within a 15km diameter part of New York with ample 'cycle-space' plus sites that can be redeveloped with a bicycling focus. Accounting for circuity the average riding distance between any two randomly selected points in this zone would be less than 10km. Access to most of the jobs in the district would take less than half an hour on average. (Calculations to come).

The Chelsea Bike-Lovers' Housing proposal provides a new future vision for the world's bellwether city, as it turns away from driving, and even walking and trains, toward a bicycle mobility platform.

# chapter 1

# Why Should We Think About Bicycling Cities?

## Sustainably Selfish

1
Kans Rosling, 'Global
Population Growth Box by
Box', TED Talk, June 2010.
Available online: http://
www.ted.com/talks/
hans_rosling_on_global_
population_growth?lan-
guage=en#t-186232

2
https://flowcharts.llnl.
gov/content/energy/
energy_archive/ener-
gy_flow_2012/2012new-
2012newUSEnergy.png.

3
https://www.cia.gov/
library/publications/
the-world-factbook/
fields/2085.html.

4
John Forester, *Effective
Cycling* (1976).

5
R. Geller, 'Four Types
of Cyclists' (Portland:
Portland Bureau of
Transportation, 2006).
Available online: http://
www.portlandoregon.
gov/transportation/
article/264746, accessed
21 May 2013.

6
Ibid, notes that only 1 per
cent of the population
would regularly and hap-
pily cycle in a city where
the roads were designed
purely with drivers in
mind.

The Swedish statistician Hans Rosling explains the world's problems simply enough for designers to start seeing solutions.[1] He breaks the world's
population into four groups: the 1 billion of us who can afford to travel by
plane; the next billion in the newly industrialized world who can just afford
to travel by car; the next 3 billion in the developing world who can barely
afford to travel by bike; and the remaining 2 billion in the third world who
would love to have bikes, but are struggling just to own shoes.

Now you can say Rosling is just using transport as an emblem for all
kinds of consumption, from mobile phones to mink coats, but our transport choices in the first world, on their own, set the planet up for disaster.
Never mind our dogs' taste for beef or all of those clothes we have only
worn once, it is our penchant for driving, and the way we design cities and
buildings to incentivize driving, that will ruin the world if those combined 5
billion walkers and cyclists all decide to follow this lifestyle as well.

Here are two graphs. The first shows that Americans' cars account
for 26.7 per cent of their nation's energy consumption, and let's not
forget that of the additional 23.9 per cent attributable to their industrial
sector a good portion of that goes towards building highways and cars.[2]

The second shows the energy use of an average Australian consumer. Before Aussies got solar panels and low-energy light bulbs,
transport was accounting for roughly a third of each person's carbon
footprint – that's all of the toes and the ball. Now, though, with those
solar panels, each is running with their heels in the air. The ball and the
toes – the portions related to transport – account for the lion's share of
their impact on global warming.

So Rosling is right. It is the example we set with our driving
that means we can't allow the world's poor to attain our economical
standing; the moment they start getting what we have the seas will rise
like they'd jumped in our bathtubs and the land we grow crops on will
be laden with salt.

But as Rosling points out we can't leave them in poverty either.
That's not just because it will make us feel guilty. It is because their birth
rates will only decline when they are sufficiently rich and well educated,
and because we don't know whether the planet can cope with a much
larger population than it has now.

The answer is easy, right? We just have to give up our cars and
meet the third-world in the middle, all riding bikes. So why don't we? It
comes back to the cities and buildings we go on creating. With millions
of kilometres of sealed roadways (4.3 million in the US alone[3]) we have
shaped our built environments to be the natural compliments to going
by car. Buildings spaced apart so that cities balloon and with ample car
parking around them are a sure-fire prescription for driving. As surely as
harbours and docks lead to boating, and stations and tracks lead to train
trips, roadways and sprawl produce driving.

There are of course individuals, the 'vehicular cyclists',[4] otherwise
known as 'the strong and fearless',[5] who ride bikes in cities designed for
the speed of the car. As a percentage of the population they account for
about 1.[6] It will take more than public awareness campaigns to make the

A TED Talk by Hans Rosling

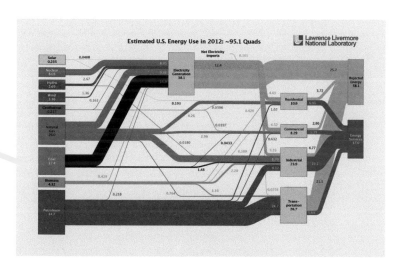

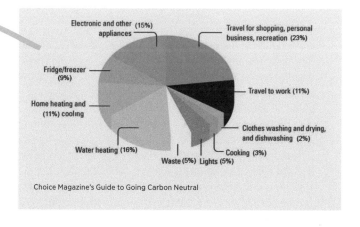

Choice Magazine's Guide to Going Carbon Neutral

7
P.N. Prins, J. Panter, J.
Heinen, S.J. Griffin, D.B.
Ogilvie, 'Causal Pathways
Linking Environmental
Change with Health Be-
haviour Change: Natural
Experimental Study of
New Transport Infrastruc-
ture and Cycling to Work',
*Preventive Medicine*, Vol.
87 (June 2016), 175-182.

other 99 per cent cycle. Typically only about 15 per cent of new ridership can ever be attributed to awareness campaigns – advertising, rider training, ride to work programs, etcetera. Behavioural change is mostly attributable to improvements in physical conditions for cycling.[7] If the world shifts to cycling it will be due to the efforts of environmental designers, not inventors of smartphone apps.

To the vehicular cyclists we can now add the smug. Recently returned to their car-centric cities from trips to the Netherlands, and now owning shiny versions of the bikes they saw when they were there, they ride at a snail's pace in carriageways just to drive motorists crazy. Their hope is their neighbours will catch the craze too. They overlook a pitfall with piety: how it isn't infectious. On the contrary, it depends on most people doing the wrong thing so the handful who do right can feel morally higher.

We need to stop hoping against hope for an awakening among the world's 2 billion drivers. For as long as we all live in and go on designing environments that anticipate driving, most of us will be drivers and each person crossing from poverty to affluence will aspire to the sprawl-and-car lifestyle.

A quick recap before moving on. Knowing that broad-based affluence and education are our best defence against a global population explosion, we are trying to bring 5 billion people out of poverty. Right now, though, that would mean introducing 5 billion more people to a car-centric model of urban development that would propel global warming.

What the world needs is an elegant, lean, regenerative model of urban development that all of us, even if we can afford cars, will choose over the car-centric city. Let it be for all the wrong reasons: more money, more sex, more time to do nothing, etcetera. The problem is not one of devising sustainable models. We have one already, the pedestrian city, the futility of which we'll discuss in a moment. What we need is a model that doesn't exist, that we have to invent, that satiates the cravings of a species we know to be selfish. What we have at the moment is a lot of talk about sustainable development while we carry on building car parking with every new building. We need a model that will regenerate the planet that we want for our selfish-worst selves.

So! To the pedestrian city! We have a wonderful example right there in New York, the city we all want to go to, or are proud to say we have lived in, no matter how briefly. With shops, schools and entertainment all within walking distance, and everything else (specialized jobs, universities and civic amenities) within 60 minutes by train (that's accounting for walking and waiting, and the likelihood of a transfer) it stands as living proof that a sustainable and enjoyable life awaits any of us who are prepared to sacrifice our yards and garages. But if it is such a great model, why have no contemporary urban developments been modelled upon it?

My wife and I spent a university semester on the Upper West Side of New York, near Columbia University, when our children were aged one and six. Having to haul kids and groceries upstairs because we weren't earning enough to rent in a building with its own elevator, and having to all ride on that god-awful train, gave us some sympathy for those traitors who flee to the suburbs the day they have kids. The urban village and its conglomerate partner, the transit-oriented city, present those raising children with a few inconveniences that can be struck out with one easy stroke. They just have to move into a house with internal garaging. So that's what most do.

Is there anything we can do to change peoples' minds? Broadcast talks by Jan Gehl on prime-time TV? Place copies of Jane Jacobs's *The Death and Life of Great American Cities* in bedside drawers in hotels? Share episodes of *Seinfeld* via Facebook with everyone we know in the suburbs? Buy Big-Hugs-Elmo toys for our nieces and nephews so they think *Sesame Street* is the address of success?

We would be wasting our time. The medium rise, high site coverage, fine-grain, walkable model with little or no reliance on cars has enjoyed more propaganda than fair-trade coffee, public schooling, seasonal fruit, Hessian shopping bags, dolphin-friendly tuna or any other socially-responsible consumer item you can name. It has money going for it as well. Wherever an eighteenth or nineteenth century urban core hasn't been butchered by car-crazed engineers you are likely to find the most expensive space per square metre in your city. An apartment without any parking in Greenwich Village – that if it were not for Jane Jacobs would now be a highway – can easily go for millions of dollars. You would think developers would want to build new Greenwich Villages all over Long Island. You would think four-storey walk-ups with no garaging would be the development model of choice throughout America's heartland.

Unfortunately the pedestrian city is just a dusted-off relic. We will gladly clean one up if it has been left to us by our non-driving ancestors. What we don't do, and won't do, is build new pedestrian cities. Our nearest approximations all have car parking hidden away. Unless a new building happens to be slap-bang in the old walkable centre of town, developers, financiers, investment buyers, even owner-occupiers, all agree parking is needed. With each new development we put a car parking strategy in place from the outset, like farmers making sure they have water.

This can leave us believing that the way to care for the planet and public health is to try to make non-driving options appealing. We devise tricks to get people to walk, bike or use public transport. If we're lucky we will end up with new urban districts where all transport options are good. We see this in Rotterdam, a city where in theory every mode wins. Rotterdam has wide roads and ample garaging, but also wide footpaths and malls for pedestrians, frequent public transport and the best of Dutch bike infrastructure and bike parking provisions. What could be wrong? The mode share. Rotterdam has as many trips by car as those other three modes put together.[8] The planet can't cope with an extra 5 billion living like that!

When residents of apartments just a few hundred metres from the centre of Rotterdam agreed to wear tracking devices as part of study at the Delft University of Technology, fewer were found to be leaving home by their buildings' front doors than by the doors to their basement garages. Worse still, many were driving straight to the same malls in the

8
Fourty-nine per cent of trips in Rotterdam are by car, 18 per cent by walking, 17 per cent by public transport and 16 per cent by bike. See: European Platform on Mobility Management (EPOMM) modal split tool, available online: http://www.epomm.eu/tems/index.phtml?-Main_ID=2928, accessed 8 April 2015.

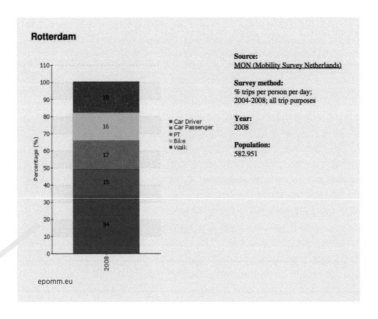

**Rotterdam**

Percentage (%)

Legend:
- Car Driver
- Car Passenger
- PT
- Bike
- Walk

2008

Values (top to bottom): 18, 16, 17, 15, 34

**Source:**
MON (Mobility Survey Netherlands)

**Survey method:**
% trips per person per day;
2004-2008; all trip purposes

**Year:**
2008

**Population:**
582.951

epomm.eu

Car-oriented development 500m from Rotterdam's walkable centre.

Regular movements of people, by car, from apartments

Ray's Indoor Mountain Bike Park, Cleveland, OH

suburbs where they had been shopping before they moved to the city.[9] City planners who lionize walking, cycling and transit, but who anticipate driving from the moment they open their sketch pads, aren't doing much more for the planet than those planning suburbs.

## Toward a Bicycle Urbanism

We have looked at three models now. First, the city for driving that will ruin the world when the rest of the world catches up. Next, the city for walking, assisted by public transport: epitomized by New York and going strong also in many eighteenth and nineteenth century urban cores, this is the model that urban evangelists have failed to sell as a paradigm for new urban growth. Lastly, the city where everyone wins, except the planet; and nobody loses, especially not the car and oil companies. Rotterdam is one of the older and larger examples of this last kind of city, but we should note that the availability of former industrial land in many cities means they are being redeveloped along similar lines.

To abate global warming we need a fourth model, one that excites the world's 2 billion drivers – or in the first instance the developed world's trendsetters. We need a model so captivating that it triggers a wave of urban experimentation such as we have not seen since the 1950s in places like Levittown. Romantics who are seduced by all new inventions might say the next wave will be inspired by the driverless car, monorail systems, travelators, or who knows what they will come up with next! This book is addressed to the person who takes Ockham's razor to problems, who can imagine the next great wave of experimentation in urban form pivoting around elegant devices, like the squeezers and peelers that are at one with our bodies in the contemporary kitchen, or the humble old pushbike.

In this enterprise there will be few lessons learned from Dutch cities like Groningen with world's highest bike modal share. That was a city that was designed in anticipation of people moving on horses or simply walking. It's medieval. The street grid and most of the buildings predate the bicycle by 600 years.[10] It tells us that bikes are a clean alternative to the horse, in a horse city, but nothing about a purpose-built bicycle city. The later, surely, would take advantage of the way bikes can be slowed by slight rises, and the fact that they don't crap on the floor when you bring them inside.

Neither should we be looking back to new towns like Milton Keynes in the U.K. or Houten in the Netherlands. To be sure, each gives bike riders terrific amenity. In Houten cyclists can ride through the centre while drivers are sent back to the ring road. But in each of these towns a lot more has been spent on infrastructure to facilitate driving than infrastructure to facilitate cycling. We can't have 5 billion more people having cities built for them like these.

This book calls for a kind of urban environment that has never been seen, one we will need to invent, that is particular to going by bike. Why the bike? Why use a knife to cut carrots and not some carrot dicing machine?

9
Jeroen van Schaick and Stefan C. van der Spek, *Urbanism on Track: Application of Tracking Technologies in Urbanism* (Amsterdam: IOS, 2008).

10
A map showing the age of every building in the Netherlands can be found online: http://code.waag.org/buildings/#52.3736,4.9013,13.

11
Dug Begley, 'Argument for Why Our Traffic Isn't That Bad, a.k.a. Hooray Cars'. Available online: http://blog.chron.com/thehighwayman/2014/09/argument-for-why-our-traffic-isnt-that-bad-a-k-a-hooray-cars/#26653101=6, accessed 15 January 2015.

12
Key funders of the leading pamphleteer for sprawl, Wendell Cox, include the Highway Users Alliance, the Heartland Institute and the Cato Institute. Cox's piece, 'Improving the Competitiveness of Metropolitan Areas', *Policy Series*, No. 135 (Winnipeg: Frontier Centre for Public Policy, 2012), typifies output that influences policy yet bypasses editorial or peer review processes. It draws conclusions (Table 8, p. 36) from the United States Census Bureau's *American Community Survey* that asks respondents how many minutes it takes them to get from home to work, most likely not capturing walking time to and from car parks.

13
When ranked according the number of jobs on offer within various commuting time bands, America's sprawling car cities fare well, but then so too does New York. See: David Levison, *Access Across America*, (Minneapolis: Centre for Transportation Studies, University of Minnesotta, 2013), 5, table 'Rank of Accessibility by Metropolitan Area 2010'.

14
Robert Cervero, 'Efficient Urbanisation: Economic Performance and the Shape of the Metropolis', *Urban Studies*, Vol. 38 (2001) No.10, 1651 -1671. Cervero's research demonstrates the strong relationship between labour accessibility and economic performance, all else being equal.

It is the most elegant and reliable tool for the task.

To date only play spaces like velodromes, indoor pump tracks and freestyle BMX parks have been designed in sympathy with the physics of cycling. These are worthy of study for the understandings they give us about the way cyclists move in spaces made especially for them, for example how riders speed between mounds and congregate on plateaus in a freestyle BMX park or comfortably traverse the cambered walls of a velodrome. Nevertheless, bicycle playgrounds are unnecessarily challenging places to ride. They demand too much skill of most bicycle users, who, let us be honest, are not on their bikes to have fun. They are riding to get some place else. Any principles we are able to distil from places built to have fun on a bike will need toning down by about 90 per cent if they are to be part of our conception of a city designed for bike transport.

Among the handful of us who regularly cycle in the first world, a significant percentage have come to see bikes as things on which to be reckless, with races or ramps. The world's poor who rely on their bikes would be appauled. Even people from affluent nations like Denmark and the Netherlands who rely on their bikes to move fast through the city are not usally so frivolous. You see in their eyes in their rush-hour columns, that most Danish and Dutch transport cyclists are interested in one thing alone: not being late. All those other benefits of cycling and of a city built for it, like the abatement of global warming, improved public health, eyes on the street, building social capital through chance interaction, and all of the money it saves, don't mean as much as improved travel times.

We see in peoples' propensity to shoulder debt for the sake of a more prestigious car or a house on the hill, that the car and sprawl model has never been harmed by its price tag. Yes, it's expensive, but worth the expense if it saves us time: time commuting each day to good jobs, time going shopping, or time spent travelling to go on a date. Put another way, the car and sprawl model promises superior access to markets: labour markets, retail markets, dating markets, etcetera.

Residents of the Dallas-Fort Worth metroplex will gladly tell you they have the shortest commute times of anyone in any city with 6 million people.[11] Cynics might say the conservative think tanks and consultants stoking such pride are sponsored by vested interests, so they must be cooking the books.[12] Still, it's unlikely they're lying too much about average commuting times in transit oriented metropolises like Tokyo, Hong Kong or Singapore being roughly an hour while in Dallas-Fort Worth they are roughly half that. The polynuclear city with elevated freeways and cloverleafs everywhere may be expensive, obesogenic, antisocial, unsustainable and a land-use fiasco, but in its purest manifestation as seen there in Texas it is a promising proposition for connecting millions of people to a wide choice of jobs, schools and shops.[13] It drives greenies crazy, but it is why the automotive city still prospers.[14]

Four of the most exciting and bewildering days of my life were spent between a hotel near the airport and down town Fort Worth when I was a scholar of the architect Louis I. Kahn. While Kahn's Kimbell Art Museum that I had gone there to study sure made an impression, I was impressed even more by the size of the billboards. They were like basketball courts turned on their sides telling me why I should take the next exit: see the biggest range of new mowers; taste someone's famous fried chicken; be sexually aroused by dozens of lap dancers on stage at this moment. At one point, when I was trying to change lanes, it dawned on me that every car had a gun in the glove box. Scanning through the radio stations all I could find were gospel songs and DJs praying with listeners who were phoning in live, in case God was listening, to say they were sick or in debt. The speedometer read 70, always, and that's *miles* per hour, not far off what you need to get lift off.

There is one thing about the metroplex, though, that is hard to fault. You might be the 6 millionth farthest person from me. You might be on the east side of Dallas, while I'm on the West side of Fort Worth. Yet within half an hour we could reach the same car park somewhere in the middle to meet face to face. No wonder there are so many lap dancers on stage at one time: a potential market of three million men are all just a short drive away.

During the whole four days I was there I only encountered one traffic jam, caused by a minor crash on the verge beside six lanes of traffic. Yes, it was annoying, but compared to my experiences with regular delays catching trains when I lived in Singapore and New York (two exemplary cities for transit), being trapped in a car for a quarter of an hour was hardly the end of the world. It gave me time to admire the billboards and wonder where on earth the food and the petrol was sent in from each day to keep this all working. Mexico and Iraq I suppose.

These days I wonder where the demand for this model of urban expansion will come from to cause it to proliferate and ruin the world. Broadly speaking: any place that doesn't have it already. The people of Africa, India and rural China are just like us. They want the most for their children, not what is modest or meek. They want whatever model of urban development appears to promise their kids the best paying jobs, no matter how ravenous, war-mongering or ultimately self-defeating that model may be. That is why they are not rioting at this moment in countries like India, where 70 per cent of their transport-infrastructure development funds are being spent on roads and flyovers while the amount being spent on the kinds of non-motorized modes that people rely on in their day-to-day lives is so small that no one is recording the figures.[15]

We should therefore be thinking of the purpose-built bicycle city as a city where people will be monetarily richer. Ignore its promise to save the planet and add years to your life. Ask if the built bicycle city has the potential to provide faster and more reliable connections for up to 6 million people, like the population of Dallas-Fort Worth.

The hypothesis is that a bicycle mobility platform is the ideal basis on which to plan a highly populated city if the goal is connection to markets. In a city designed especially for cycling, the naturally low viscosity of bicycle traffic (the way bikes flow through tight gaps) and the possibility of riding into buildings, along corridors and all the way to your kitchen or your office desk, are the qualities that can be exploited to make the fastest kind of city yet seen. A bike may only be one fifth as fast as a car,

15
See: Mark Brussell and Mark Zuidgeest, 'Cycling in Developing Countries: Context, Challenges and Policy Relevant Research', in: J. Parkin (Ed.), *Cycling and Sustainability* (Bingley: Emerald, 2012), 181-218. Available online: http://books.google.com.au/books?hl=en&lr=&id=HUL-vxkRatT8C&oi=fnd&pg=PP1&dq=john+parkin+cycling+and+sustainability&ots=G_PtE7FvL5&sig=hJwL-WntSBkxCwc0JxZDBM-0MKQIQ#v=onepage&q=-john%20parkin%20cycling%20and%20sustainability&f=false, accessed 9 April 2015.

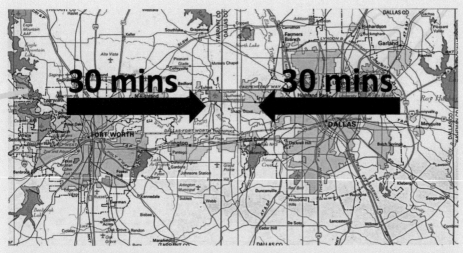

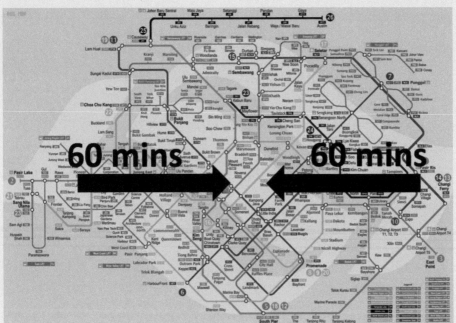

The time it takes drivers on opposite sides of Dallas-Fort Worth to meet mid way, verses the time similar journeys take transit users in Singapore. Both cities have populations of roughly six million. Furthermore Dallas's road network handles 90% of all trips, where Singapore's public transport system only needs to serve a portion of the population who can't afford cars.

but bicycling traffic is more than five times as slippery. Remember my story from Texas, how six lanes of car traffic could not merge into five to pass a crash on the verge. In cities like Amsterdam and Utrecht you can see bicycle traffic can flow through the eye of a needle. And where motorists spend considerable time walking to their end destinations from wherever they have to park (time not reliably captured in travel time studies[16]) renegades among us know that bike trips needn't stop at the bike rack. We can ride all the way to the room we are heading to.

Progressive urban theorists are prone to eschew the notion of speed. In the context of a car city, it has been the enemy of everything good: community, nature, 'people'. Talking down the importance of speed has been the first step toward talking the other three up. There are some problems here, though. One is that the value of speed, or *connection* speed (a concept we have all come to understand better since getting the internet) is vital to the competitiveness of a city. Another is that rational thinking itself, which just so happens to be the agent of speed in the engineer's paradigm, can be unfairly viewed as a bully. It is an inductive fallacy to argue that rationality, just because it happens to be employed in the service of travel times, should become the thing we start blaming for the car and sprawl model.

If rationality had been properly employed by avant-garde designers of cities in the 1920s and 1930s, someone would have pointed out that the car itself is an irrational tool, that it has two motors when it only needs one. One of those motors, the driver's body, has the special quality of getting stronger with use. Yet this is the motor left idle in this design. The motor that wears out the more it is used, the one made of steel, is the one that sends power back to the wheels. If the car were rationalized – for example, stripped of non-essentials – it would grow pedals and lose the steel motor.

Many have remarked on the dearth of rationality among architects in the early days of the machine age who fancied themselves as masters of reason. It has been said, for example, that Antonio Sant'Elia, the first of the futurist architects, was 'uninformed' in the way he 'endowed his imaginary machine-made metropolis with mythical attributes of speed and omnipotence'.[17] Esther da Costa Meyer likens him to his romantic forebears gazing at mountains, though in this case gazing at big machines. We can go further, though. It is fair to say that Sant'Elia, Ludwig Hilberseimer, Harvey Wiley Corbett, Le Corbusier and other architects at the dawn of the machine age would have imagined the city of the future quite differently had they not been romantics, but the arch rationalists they purported to be. Had they been rational, not romantic, they would have been taking about the rational need of optimize connection speeds between people, not the isolated and purposeless challenge of allowing cars to go faster in cities.

[16]
The travel time surveys the author was able to access in researching this book do not make it clear where journey times start and stop. For instance the American Community Survey simply asks 'How many minutes did it usually take this person to get from home to work last week?'. United States Census Bureau, *Commuting in the United States: 2009* (U.S. Department of Commerce, September 2011).

[17]
Esther da Costa Meyer, *The Work of Antonio Sant'Elia: Retreat into the Future* (New Haven: Yale University Press, 1995).

## Hypothetical Speed Verses Speed of Connection

18
Eric W. Weisstein, 'Disk
Line Picking', *MathWorld
– Wolfram Web Resource*.
Available online: http://
mathworld.wolfram.com/
DiskLinePicking.html,
accessed 9 April 2015.

We can thank the internet for giving us all a better appreciation of connection speeds, as opposed to absolute speeds. When we first started
using it in the 1990s we marvelled at how bits of information were
crossing oceans in less than a second. Soon, though, we were frustrated
at the time it was taking for image files to pass through our modems.
Having learned from that experience, we are less inclined now to marvel
at the way new fibre-optic cables can courier high-definition movies from
one side of the world to the other in seconds. What we want to know is
whether that data will need to be schlepped through coaxial cables from
node points outside of our homes. We are more concerned about the
speed of that data over the last few metres than over an entire ocean.

The car city is like a fibre-to-node network, distributing our bodies
across vast distances at speeds 25 times faster than we are able to walk,
but putting lead in our boots just when we are tantalizingly close to our
destinations. Even if we are lucky and avoid any jams, we are guaranteed
of having to walk, probably with our bags in our hands, from wherever
we eventually managed to park.

In the case of cities, like Tokyo or Hong Kong, that depend upon
public transport, walking time to and from nodes (stations) and the chaos
surrounding those nodes are also examples of this. The most maddening
thing is sitting on a train that keeps stopping at nodes of no interest to us.

What options remain? As a thought experiment we can imagine
designing a city for millions where everyone walks. It would mean fore-
going the 25-fold increase in speed we get with a car once it is on the
expressway, or a train when it is midway between stations, for the 3-5
kph speed of a person on foot. For you and I to meet in the middle in half
an hour, as we could if starting from opposite sides of Dallas-Fort Worth,
this imaginary city of walkers could be no more than 5-km across, or 20
square kilometres in area.

How dense would it need to be to accommodate millions? As dense
as Manhattan? Tokyo? How about Kowloon Walled City, Hong Kong's
notorious slum? We're not even close. The densities required might draw
the earth into the sun. There wouldn't be room to sleep lying down.

So here is another thought experiment. Imagine the buildings of
Manhattan elevated off of the ground on pilotis. Imagine no cars, only
bikes making beelines all over the ground plane. Now imagine your new
raised-off-the-ground version of Manhattan changing from its sausage
shape into the shape of a 15-km-wide circle – that's a significant increase
in its overall size. What you are imagining now is a city with the same
population as Dallas-Fort Worth where trip times are faster, and more
reliably so. For now let's think in pure mathematical terms. We'll come
back and factor in zig-zagging and how people prefer jobs, schools and
shops that are closer to home.

Using something known as 'disc line picking' [18] and this formula

$$d = 128r/45\pi$$

it can be ascertained that the average distance (d) between any two
randomly selected points on a 15-km-wide disc is 6.79 km. Assuming

Kowloon Walled City

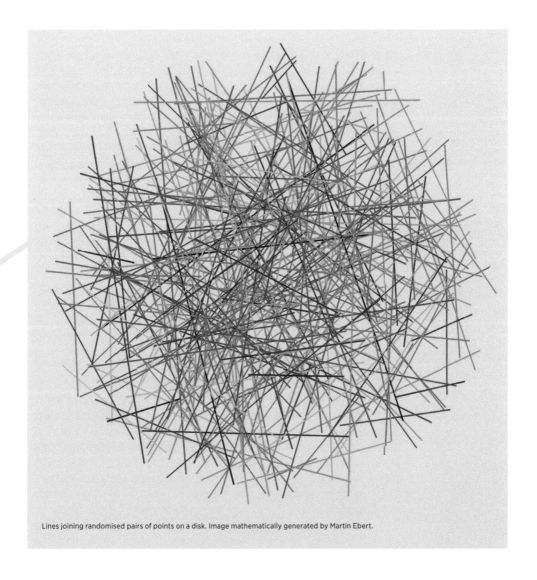

Lines joining randomised pairs of points on a disk. Image mathematically generated by Martin Ebert.

19
David J.C. MacKay, Sus-
tainable Energy – Without
the Hot Air (Cambridge:
UIT Cambridge, 2009),119.

jobs and population densities are evenly distributed across our imaginary 15-km-wide city, 6.79 km would be the average length trip. Travelling at 15 kph, the speed one can cycle with no more effort than walking,[19] in an uninterrupted beeline, that trip would take 27 minutes and 9 seconds, slightly less than the reported average commutes in Dallas-Fort Worth. Alternatively, if we set out from opposite sides and rode toward one another at 15 kph, we would meet in the middle in half an hour.

Better still, we would not have to meet in a car park in order to achieve that record time. Meeting in a café or office in Dallas-Fort Worth could easily add ten minutes to each of our trips – you know, those ten minutes when we send each other those all too predictable texts: 'sorry, had to park miles away' or 'just buying a ticket to put on the dashboard' or 'just getting change for the meter'. In a purpose-built bicycle city we would both arrive at our actual rendezvous point, still on our bikes. How? By ensuring bicycle planning does not stop at a building's front door. Neither should it stop at the architecturally designed bike parking station. Bicycle planning can carry into the plan of each building.

Devising a sustainable model of urban development with the potential to woo the first-world, and therefore the other five billion, will mean some clever design strokes aimed at shaving off time lost in travel. Any new urban model has to save us time to reach boardrooms, seats in cafés, the actual stations or desks where we work, the store aisles where we shop and the pantries to which we return after shopping, not just the time it takes to reach parking nodes. Pregnant within that proposition is the necessity of planning the interiors of buildings around bicycle motion. That seems outlandish given interiors have been designed around walking since Mycenae, Harappa and Abydos. However, those are the kinds of lengths we should consider to shake people out of this spell they are under, believing the car city and its own set of proprietary buildings (free-standing housing with internal garaging, shopping mall parking lots, drive-through restaurant, etcetera) all save them time in their day.

The task is made easier by the rise of universal design principles, thanks to which architects are already required to provide wheeled access to most parts of most public buildings. It is made harder by two things. One is the idea that old horse cities exemplify best practice when it comes to building for bikes. Take Copenhagen, with a relatively imper-meable grid of very large blocks, funnelling streets leading to an under-supply of bridges for the river and lakes and buildings that you can't take a bike inside. People on bikes may have barrier protection from cars, but they lose time by having to share streets with cars in the first place. They lose even more time zigzagging past giant blocks when a perme-able street grid would let them take shorter routes. They lose time again when stopping to lock up their bikes and detach luggage, and again as they walk into buildings. They lose time faffing with raingear because Copenhagen's patrons of bicycle transport, unlike the city's motorists and patrons of public transport, aren't provided with weather protection as they could easily be if porticos or canopies were built over their bike paths. A few days' earnings per year is spent just to cover the cost of insuring their bikes in a city where thieves can wander unchecked among bike racks outdoors. If Copenhagen were a purpose-built bicycling city, and not just a city where bikes are accommodated, all those problems would have been struck out by design.

Our other obstacle is an historical echo between the kind of propositions presented herein and those of discredited visionaries of the interwar period – Geoffrey Jellicoe, Ludwig Hilberseimer, Harvey Wiley Corbett, etcetera – with their larger than life renderings of new building types that integrated road infrastructure. Drawings by British motoring artist Bryan de Grineau are some of the wildest. They illustrate recommendations for London by Charles Bressey, Britain's Chief Engineer for Roads in the 1920s and 1930s. What we're seeing, really, is a snapshot of a time when the rush to bring cars into cities was so welcome it muzzled critique. No one asked about the logic of highways benefitting everyone *except* for the people whose houses would act as supports in de Grineau's and Bressey's vision. No one asked who would want to occupy space that flanked roadways on the faces of buildings. It is clear no one thought through the consequences of the grand plan succeeding and causing millions of cars to flood into our cities.

The visions in this book are different. If you just look at the pictures and ignore the accompanying text, then yes, you will be reminded of interwar modernist madness. That is not how this book is laid out, though. For every design proposition you will find a discussion of the assumptions that have kept urban design trapped in a political impasse for the past 50 years.

## Suspicion of Machines among Today's Gentry

The late 1960s saw a sharp turn away from mechanical engineering and all the wonderful things it had been doing for humanity since the time of Leonardo da Vinci. One indicator of an impending cultural turn was the 1968 exhibition 'The Machine as Seen at the End of the Mechanical Age' at the Museum of Modern Art in New York.[20] We can understand bell-wethers like the MoMA wanting to get the jump on the rest by being the first to say something is ending, but really, 1968? That's one year before Neil Armstrong stepped on the moon. Wasn't that a little too early to be speaking of the mechanical age in the past tense?

Not really. Reading Matthew Tribbe's *No Requiem for the Space Age*, we get a sense that 1968 was just about right.[21] Tribbe's retrospective reveals how cheering for the space race was fading even before the race was won, and how just one year after Neil Armstrong walked on the moon most Americans could not even remember his name. In fact, on the eve of the lunar landing, the pioneer aviator Charles Lindbergh was refusing to comment on what NASA was about to achieve, telling *Time* magazine that the frontier we really ought to be exploring was personal awareness, something we would not be able to reach in a rocket.

Back issues of *Time* are only one place to go looking for signs of a cultural turn. They might not be so obvious, but records of architectural discourse

20
Pontus Hultén, *The Machine, As Seen at the End of the Mechanical Age* (New York: The Museum of Modern Art,1968).

21
Matthew Tribbe, *No Requiem for the Space Age: The Apollo Moon Landings and American Culture* (New York: Oxford University Press, 2014).

Bryan de Grineau and Charles Bressey's vision for London

Neil Armstrong on the moon

Davies's book High Tech Architecture

Color-coded ducting of the Patscentre, New Jersey

are another. It has been the case since Leon Battista Alberti's *Ten Books* that architects' theories have been thinly disguised sales pitches to prospective clients.[22] If we are still reading their theories today it is because those architects' words struck a note with their patrons. What we often forget is patrons' real interest in architectural discourse, how these days for instance, they buy monographs and attend architects' talks.

In addition to treatises, the would-be patron also has criticism and scholarship to keep abreast of. What would patrons be hoping to find by following all of this discourse? Assurance, presumably, that they are not paying millions for mere bricks and mortar. For that kind of money they want their worldviews reflected, not just by any old architect, but ones whose theories are discussed positively by the critics.

The Austrian art and architectural historian Emil Kaufmann takes the next logical step, arguing that the significance of art and architectural theory, 'does not reside in the fact that it points the way for its own age, but in its serving subsequent generations as a monument to past ideas.'[23] In other words, the eventual and most rewarded consumers of theory are historians looking back on it. Old copies of *Time* might reveal the mood of the masses, but past architectural discourse gives us a window on the aspirations and tastes of an important societal class: the class who are holding the chequebooks. For convenience sake, let's call them the gentry.

What can we gather about the gentry's feelings toward the mechanical age from past architectural discourse? Judging by the critical backlash toward 1980s British hi-tech architecture, we would have to say machine love in architecture had its last sputter with Richard Rogers and Norman Foster. No architects or clients in their right mind would want a repeat dose of the wrath that 1980s hi tech suffered from critics. Let's look at what three of them said, starting with Colin Davies, who should not have been a critic at all.

Normally when a book bears the title of an architectural movement it opens with glowing descriptions of that movement's exponents, main works and ideas. Davies's book *High Tech Architecture* isn't like that.[24] The introduction is more like a list of reasons to buy the next book on the shelf, not one about a movement with such a host of logical flaws. But with his reputation worth more than book sales, Davies wasn't about to gloss over the problems.

Given Michael Sorkin's reputation, criticism is not so surprising. All he has ever needed is fodder. He found some of his best ever in the hi-tech architects' way of colour coding services ducts the way engineers colour code these in their working drawings. This provided Sorkin with one of the most damning lines in architectural criticism since St Augustine described Adam's garden: 'Useless information marshalled with bone-headed rigor signifying nothing beyond the act of signification.'[25]

Charles Jencks spent the 1980s lampooning hi-tech architecture, so was bound to hit the nail on the head a few times. It is not that hi-tech buildings have any more problems, he argued in 1990, but that 'people feel let down when, inevitably, some mechanisms fail'.[26] Here Jencks captured the central problem with hi-tech architecture in a way that any of us

22
Leon Battista Alberti, On the Art of Building in Ten Books, translated by Joseph Rykwert, Neil Leach and Robert Tavernor (Cambridge, MA: MIT Press, 1988).

23
Cited in: Hanno-Walter Kruft, A History of Architectural Theory (New York: Princeton Architectural Press, 1994).

24
Colin Davies, High Tech Architecture (London: Thames and Hudson, 1988).

25
Michael Sorkin, 'Another Low-Tech Spectacular', in: Michael Sorkin (Ed.). Exquisite Corpse: Writings on Buildings (New York: Verso, 1991 [1985]), 131.

26
Charles Jencks, The New Moderns: From Late to Neo-Modernism (New York: Rizzoli, 1990).

27
Catherine Cooke,
'Russian Precursors', in:
*Deconstruction: Omnibus
Volume*, Andreas Papa-
dakis, Catherine Cooke
and Andrew Benjamin
(Eds.) (London: Academy
Editions, 1989), 11-12.

28
Erik Brynjolfsson and
Andrew McAfee, *The
Second Machine Age:
Work, Progress, and Pros-
perity in a Time of Brilliant
Technologies* (New York:
W. W. Norton & Company,
2014).

29
Op. cit. (note 27), 11.

30
Kenneth Frampton,
'Towards a Critical
Regionalism: Six Points
for an Architecture of
Resistance', in: Hal Foster
(Ed). *Postmodern Culture*
(London: Pluto Press,
1989).

31
Sigfried Giedion, *Space,
Time and Architecture: The
Growth of a New Tradition*
(Cambridge, MA: Harvard
University Press, 1941).

32
Colin St John Wilson,
*Other Tradition of Modern
Architecture: The Uncom-
pleted Project* (London:
Black Dog Publishing,
1995).

who has ever paid money for a machine that broke down can relate to.

It would be interesting to hear Jencks's thoughts about the light regulating panels in the Arab World Institute in Paris. These stopped working in 2011 and will cost too much even for an oil-rich client to fix. Millions of dollars' worth of mechanical irises are now sitting frozen, telling exactly how cloudy it was the moment the whole system failed.

The Spanish inquisition brought on by their love of mechanical claptrap would eventually cause hi-tech architects to tone down the engineers' colour coding and the adornment of exteriors with structure and apparatus. There are fewer glass elevators on the outside of buildings these days, far fewer exterior ducts, and no more of those permanent cranes on the roof to shuffle the ductwork. The kinds of technological totems we are left with are ones that will probably pay their own way, like solar and wind power generators.

The really valuable thing about hi-tech architecture is it forced architectural theorists to firm up their positions with regards to the mechanical engineering paradigm. This was evident in discussions about the next major movement, deconstructionism. In the 1989 book she co-authored regarding this movement, architectural theorist Catherine Cooke observed that Western society had entered 'the second machine age', the age of information technology.[27] When you consider that it took until 2014 for Erik Brynjolfsson and Andrew McAfee to use *The Second Machine Age* as the title and thesis of a mass-market book, Cooke's remark was precocious.[28]

1989 was not too early, though, for Cooke to declare that anyone employing the same thought processes to design cities and buildings that one might use to design a machine would be a throwback to an earlier age defined by the *konstruktsia* method of thinking about social structures and buildings. This is what Russian constructivist architects had promoted in the hope socialism would work like a well-oiled machine. According to Cooke this is an entirely inappropriate way of thinking in 'the age of information technology, where space, as Tschumi said, is measured by time.'[29]

In the same year that Cooke was saying we have to drop the machine as a model and mechanical engineering as a model of thinking, Kenneth Frampton was arguing for something he called a 'critical *arrière-garde* position'. He didn't think architects should be nostalgic for pre-industrial times. He just thought they should distance themselves from 'the Enlightenment myth of progress' and separate architecture from the business of optimizing advanced technology.[30]

Colin St John Wilson joined Frampton's cause with a revisionist history about the way hagiographers of flat-roofed white buildings, in particular Sigfried Giedion,[31] had assiduously edited Alvar Aalto out of their books.[32] Aalto was just too much of an anomaly to the stories they wanted to tell about the machine age. A new light was shone upon what he titled *The Other Tradition of Modern Architecture*. We learned, for example, that the *arrière-garde* disposition toward technology that Frampton had just started promoting, and that any of us can sympathize with if we're cautious about paying for new kinds of machines, had been there in architectural theory since Aalto.

Arab World Institute in Paris. Photo: Zandrikuun

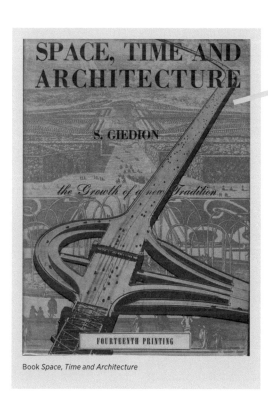

Book *Space, Time and Architecture*

Villa Savoye Le Corbusier

Alvar Aalto

Aalto's Muuratsalo Experimental House

Rem Koolhaas' *Elements* show

The orthodox modernist tradition, the one that Giedion was documenting as it occurred, has its main emblems in Le Corbusier's Villa Savoye and the motorways celebrated on the cover of Giedion's book. If a similar emblem had to be picked for the other tradition, it would probably be Aalto's Muuratsalo Experimental House.

Le Corbusier's love of machines is expressed in his villa's machine-like appearance and the pilotis that lift it up from the earth so that cars can park under. Alto's ambivalence toward the machine age is expressed by handmade brick walls and the building's transport connection back to the town: it was designed to be reached in a boat (but of course now that suburbia is pressing against it, most people drive there).

The gentry do more than just eavesdrop on conversations about the way forward for architecture. They chime in with their chequebooks. In this way they joined in the discussions chronicled above with a 'no' in the late 1980s to more buildings that paraded machinery, a 'yes' to deconstructionism with its corruption of the engineer's rational mindset and more recently a big 'yes' to the phenomenological movement in architecture, the camp of Juhani Pallasmaa, Peter Zumthor, Richard Leplastrier, Steven Holl, Rick Joy, etcetera.

Following in the tradition of Aalto, the phenomenologists' idiom emphasizes tactile jointing and planes made from natural materials like wood, brick and stone, while downplaying machinery and machine-made materials. The aim is to bring users to an awareness of their 'being-in-the-world', a Heideggerian concept[33] that Christian Norberg-Schulz borrowed in formulating the movement.[34]

Most of the European and Australasian works in *The Phaidon Atlas of 21st Century World Architecture* lean toward this camp in some way.[35] If we narrow our focus and just look at small works, we see the tropes of phenomenological architecture have taken over the whole of the globe. Since the clients are the ones who eavesdropped on the discourse, and who nodded in agreement when they opened their chequebooks, we can surmise that many aspire to 'being-in-the-world' – the *natural* world, not the world of machines.

We can't argue that there is a zeitgeist, and like Jean-François Lyotard should be sceptical of any meta-narrative according to which all architecture will one day be directing users' attention to nature and natural materials and that machines are on their way out.[36] What we can say is that the critical *arrière-garde* disposition toward mechanisation that is evident in contemporary architecture expresses the collective wisdom of today's gentry.

There are outlier voices, of course. Rem Koolhaas certainly doesn't tow Frampton's line. The message of the 'Elements of Architecture' exhibition he curated at the 2014 Venice Biennale was that smart technology is poised to bring about some significant leaps in the ways we think about every element, from doorways to floors, and that architects need to be alive to new ways these elements might all be reassembled when networked sensors have changed them. Physical doors could become electronically monitored thresholds that sound an alarm, or give you a

**33**
For Heidegger's reflections on architecture see: Martin Heidegger, 'Building, Dwelling, Thinking', in: David Farell Krell (Ed.), *Basic Writings: Martin Heidegger* (London: Routledge,1993).

**34**
For a succinct sample of Norberg-Schulz's writing on phenomenology in architecture see: Christian Norberg-Schulz, 'The Phenomenology of Place', in: Kate Nesbitt (Ed.), *Theorizing a New Agenda for Architecture* (New York: Princeton Architectural Press, 1996).

**35**
Editors of Phaidon, *The Phaidon Atlas of 21st Century World Architecture* (London: Phaidon, 2008).

**36**
Lyotard defined post-modernism as a suspicion of meta-narratives. See: Jean-François Lyotard, *The Postmodern Condition: A Report on Knowledge*, translated by Geoff Bennington and Brian Massumi (Minneapolis: University of Minnesota Press, 1984).

zap. Floors might generate power when we walk, or dance, on them.

What must be said is there was nothing about Koolhaas's show that celebrated machinery for its own sake; no lifts on the outside that would be more logically placed on the inside; no equivalents of a trip to the moon to say that we can. Overwhelmingly the show was about networked sensors (emblems of what Cooke calls the second machine age), and replacing heavy machines that were invented for buildings in the late 1800s with ingenious ones that are a fraction of the size, but which do a lot more.

A picture has emerged from this brief summary of a new sobriety among architects when they look at machines. Before a machine is invited to be a part of a building, it must pass at least one of three tests: 1) it must promise environmental dividends; or 2) it must ingeniously do a lot with a little; or 3) it must add to the data cloud in ways that might come in handy. If a machine doesn't do at least one of these, it is likely to be discarded as a nuisance distraction to our higher aim of reconnecting with the world through our senses.

But here is the problem. We can express this worldview with individual buildings, like Aalto's Muuratsalo Experimental House, or Rick Joy's Amangiri Resort and Spa. But those buildings will only ever be islands. Most of the world's surface has been organized around transport machines from the naïve early days of the machine age. People aren't rowing to Aalto's house. They are not hiking to Rick Joy's resort. In both cases they are going by car. Buildings that stand for the passing of the first machine age, rely on the very machine that emblemizes the machine age for their transport connections.

Now here is a proposal. The same design thinking that makes a post-machine age house so elegant and wise in its critical arrière-garde use of machinery, can be applied to the production of space. It should be possible to move around cities as elegantly as we move within highly regarded contemporary houses.

## SimpliCITY (Less Mess is More)

A century ago, during the First World War and its immediate aftermath, it wasn't clear which of the new mobility platforms (rail, driving or cycling) would help cities keep growing. At times it looked as though all three might become equal players; indeed, if you talk to mobility consultants they will say giving populations multiple choice is still the ideal.

No one told town planners that, though. In their production of new urban space (whether through green-field expansion or with development control plans to guide old cities into new shapes) cycling was completely overlooked in favour of mechanical forms of mobility.

Town planners have many levers on transport, but let's remind ourselves of the obvious ones: requiring car parking with each new building approval; permitting new subdivisions contingent upon the construction of major roads; or, if they want to steer people to transit, permitting higher densities within walking distance of tram routes or train stations. What is more, these levers work. All the cities that town planners have modified, or built from scratch, really do rely on whatever machines they imagined would haul the most people around. We know planners have overlooked cycling by the miniscule fractions of bike trips in any planned city, a factor of cycling being treated as an enthusiasts' pastime, rather than a mainstream mode of transportation.

Planners are like King Midas. Every city they touch turns to some golden machine – the car, the tram, the subway – until finally they look with King Midas's shame on a city where no one can move. Any little breakdown in any of the thousands of interdependent machines they planned their city around routinely brings the whole place to a standstill.

There is an alternative. Here are two screen shots from a British Pathé newsreel of 1923 Copenhagen, a time just after horses, but just before traffic lights.[37] The most striking revelation one takes from the footage is that none of the cyclists are stopping. The film affords a rare glimpse of a place and a time when point-to-point trips could be made at the full cruising speed of the transport devices that people were using. Any-one accustomed to riding a bike in the city would understand why. As a device the bike is so closely attuned to the body that it is almost as agile. Yet at the same time it can propel you, comfortably seated, at the speed of a world champion runner. Of course a bike is not as fast as a car on open roads. Where it is fast, is in the tight situations that characterize the urban mobility challenge. That is what makes cycling inherently faster than driving in cities.

The imagination can run wild with street scenes like these. Imagine the few cars, and any horses off-camera, all taken away. Had Copenhage-ners thought to ban all things noxious that required the street to be an out-door environment, shop keepers of the 1920s might have extended their awnings until they met mid-way between buildings on opposite sides of the street. They could have turned their streets into glass-roofed arcades.

Then what? Arcade floors can be tiled. The cyclists you see in those 1923 images of Copenhagen might have acquired a non-porous and fric-tionless surface to roll on. Dismiss this kind of thinking as fantasy, if you must, but do so based on aesthetics, not because you think a city with no fast machines would be too slow for commuting, taking children to school or shopping.

It's time to return to the earlier thought experiment and ask what kinds of average commute times can realistically be achieved using bikes. You will recall the experiment started with a circular city with a 15-km diameter, which if it were populated in the same way as Manhattan, would house 6 million people, as many as Dallas-Fort Worth. We're not talking about a large geographical area. If we disregard post-Second World War sprawl, few industrial cities measure more than 15 km from one side to the other.

We have ascertained that the average straight-line distance between randomly selected pairs of points in a 15-km wide city would be 6.79 km. But ground transportation can't follow straight lines. Buildings will block the way somehow. In the worst case, where one's destination is diagonally disposed to an orthogonal grid, the straight-line distance

37
'Cycle Town (1923)'.
Available online: http://
www.britishpathe.com/
video/cycle-town/query/
copenhagen, accessed
25 July 2014.

British Pathe newsreel, Cycle Town

Cyclist inside Galleria Vittoria Emanuele II, Milan

Random beelines drawn over Barcelona

Screenshots Google Earth 15km

could be multiplied by as much as the square root of two. That's a 41 per cent increase. Let us think, though, of a city with small blocks, wide streets and chamfered corners, like the Eixample district in Barcelona, and imagine cyclists being given the full width of the road easement to ride on. The impact wouldn't be half as profound. Also, a fully diagonal traverse is the worst case scenario. The best case is a straight trip. The average case is an angle of incidence of 22.5 degrees. So let's factor up the 6.79-km average distance by 18 per cent to a nice figure of 8 km.

38
Op. cit. (note 19).

Next let's factor that distance downward to account for people's inclina-tion to choose places of work that are closer to home, or homes that are closer to their places of work. From a transport planning perspective a city is thought to be doing exceptionally well if people have fast access to two out of every three available jobs. We can therefore repeat all our sums looking at two-thirds of the original area. The effect on all of the linear distances of a one-third reduction in area would be a one-fifth reduction in length. Average commute distances would therefore drop from 8 km to 6.4 km.

Fifteen kph is the speed a bike goes with the same amount of effort it takes just to walk.[38] For the purposes of trip-time calculations in a city where we are assuming there are hardly any machines on the ground plane (maybe just a few electric carts limited to 15 kph serving as mini buses and a police car or two) 15 kph would not only be the top speed for lazy cyclists, but their average speed too. That is because there would never be an occasion when anyone on a bike would have to slow down. The blocks would be small. There would be no cars stuck at traffic lights. There wouldn't *be* traffic lights! Bike traffic would be completely dispersed.

What we're imagining is a city with average commute times of 25 minutes and 36 seconds, and seeing how more of us are living more and more of our lives close to home anyway, we can guess average trip times (as opposed to average times commuting to work) would be significantly shorter again. We're looking at a way we might build the most effective mega-city for connecting people to markets. That is the reason cities exist and why we don't all live on tropical islands.

The modelling may be clumsy and there may be questions in some people's minds about the draconian lengths that would be required to clear city streets of all cars, but the tantalizing promise remains of the most connected city the world has yet seen, being so precisely because machines of connection are nearly all gone. Why wasn't this thought of in the late 1900s when bikes were more available than public transport or cars? What led us to accept that being shunted in trains or stuck in traffic is just part of the deal if we live in a city, when perhaps all we have to do to make fast, healthy, green cities is remove encumbrances to bicycle transport from the ground plane and contain sprawl?

Maybe we can forgive current town planners for never entertaining the possibility, acquiescing as they must to the short-sightedness of their con-temporaries and those in the past who left them bad legacies. But what about the conceptual thinkers? Ebenezer Howard wrote *Garden Cities*

39
Ebenezer Howard, *Garden Cities of To-morrow* (London: S. Sonnenschein & Co., 1902).

40
Ian Carlton, 'Histories of Transit-Oriented Development: Perspectives on the Development of the TOD Concept', Institute of Urban & Regional Development, University of California Berkeley (2009). Available online: https://escholarship.org/uc/item/7wm9t8r6, accessed 15 June 2014.

*of To-Morrow* during the bicycling boom of the late 1890s.[39] How could he have overlooked the potential of point-to-point bicycle transport and given his mind rather to the contemplation of a spoke-and-hub model, the precursor of transit-oriented development (TOD)?[40] And what about Le Corbusier? He is known to have liked cycling himself, so knew the bike's comfort and speed. Why did his ideal city plans revolve around cars?

We can understand why Howard doesn't consider bike transport if we put ourselves on the streets of the late 1800s. Three things were at play to make bicycle transport unthinkable as a mode for the masses. The industrial revolution was making cities much bigger and denser, authorities were playing catch-up with their rubbish collection and sewer services and logistics was still dependent on horse-drawn buggies. These factors combined meant streets in Howard's time were ankle deep in manure. This was, after all, the era that saw the invention of shopping arcades like Galerie du Palais-Royal in Paris and Galleria Vittorio Emanuele II in Milan, built as tolerable places for the *flâneur* when the street often wasn't. It was also the time of the horse-drawn omnibus that, while crowded and hardly any faster than walking, at least got its passengers above all the horse poo. In Howard's mind the bike was something to take out on macadamized roads in the country, as well-to-do cycling enthusiasts were in the habit of doing on weekends. It wasn't the way to travel to work in an office.

Where Howard was writing a fraction too soon, when city streets were a bog, Le Corbusier was writing just a little too late when cars were already an exciting new presence in Paris. The 1920s *might* have been the right time for Le Corbusier's eyes to be opened to the possibilities of bicycle transport, had he only been based further north. Had he been based in the lowlands of the Netherlands or in Denmark, he would have been exposed to the model of urban mobility mentioned above, which those countries had for a short time before the advent of traffic lights, and which has only been seen since in China.

If only Le Corbusier had been Danish or Dutch! He might have thought to couple the kind of point-to-point, on-demand, smooth flowing transport we see in that 1923 clip of Copenhagen with his idea of elevating buildings on pilotis to facilitate beelines. His towers-in-a-park model would have afforded unrivalled mobility. His mistake was putting in cars.

We're not about to start building towers-in-parks as the previous generation did in the 1960s. All we are doing right now is holding a simple idea in our minds. We are imaging a hypothetical city, a dense one, with no cars twirling overhead on ribbons of concrete, no heavy rail or light rail and no transport interchanges where taxis meet buses and trains. We are also imagining a very permeable ground plane with some combination of short chamfered blocks, shortcuts and pilotis.

The great irony is that by removing transport machines capable of reaching high speeds, there is a possibility of reducing average commuting times to 25 minutes and discretionary short trips to less time than most people waste just finding a car park.

We have also applied a kind of thinking that we trust in every field of design, except for when it comes to designing our cities. Unlike our

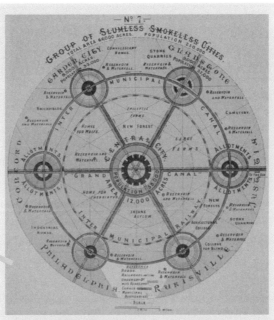

Ebeneza Howard's diagram for Garden Cities is an early precursor of the Transit Oriented Development model that is now mainstream.

c.1900 New York

Riding above the manure

Rush hour in Shanghai in 1991.
Photo by Reuters/China Daily

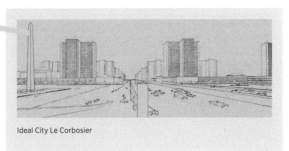

Ideal City Le Corbosier

Philippe Starck Juicer

New York first subway

parents' generation who leapt to buy electric can openers, mechanical armchairs and beds with built-in clock radios, our generation displays a preference for mortars and pestles, or beds with no features except for well-crafted joints. The most coveted juicer on the market, from Philippe Starck, has no moving parts except for the user's own arm.

Ludwig Mies van der Rohe's aphorism 'less is more' roughly captures our sensibility. 'Less mess is more', perhaps captures it better. Dieter Rams's final principle of good design seems applicable too: *'Good design is as little design as possible.* Less, but better – because it concentrates on the essential aspects, and the products are not burdened with non-essentials. Back to purity, back to simplicity.'[41]

We have learned too that more complex designs have a more limited range of possible uses, whereas the simpler the design the more likely it will be that people will find unintended and valuable uses. Complicating cities with single-use infrastructure – freeways, subways, light-rail, escalators, bus/car/train interchanges, etcetera – ends up just thwarting elementary modes like walking and cycling, and who knows what else it might thwart in the future? Frictionless skateboards? New kinds of wheelchairs? Land sailing devices?

The tenor of city planners' ongoing obsession with carriages and ever-geekier ways of moving them around is evident if we look at an interval from the dawn of this enterprise. In New York a key moment came in 1869 when Alfred Beach built that city's first subway.[42] Beach's real aim was not to solve a mobility crisis. If that had been the case he would have developed a system with large enough carriages to move thousands of people, like London's first underground steam train that had just been completed. Better still, he could have built ferry wharves. Instead he built a pneumatic tube to show how a principle used to post documents in cylindrical canisters could be enlarged to move a few people. The whole line was less than 100 m in length and remained New York's only subway until 1904. That's 35 years!

It was technology for technology's sake, unjustifiable in terms of need, but understandable if we think about the way industrialists of the time were conflating the sublimity of the American (and Australian, South African and Canadian) landscapes with a new sense of the sublime, not only conferred upon rugged cliffs and dark clouds, but on machines too. Leo Marx writes about this in *The Machine in the Garden*.[43]

While Alfred Beach's gadget was eventually demolished, gadgetry itself rebounded like the Hydra, this time with nine heads: cars, buses, taxis, motorbikes, trucks, expressways, harbour tunnels, cloverleafs and ever-widening carriageways. And today, before those heads can be severed, more heads are sprouting: Mass Rapid Transport (MRT), Personal Rapid Transport (PRT), Personal Mobility Devices (PMDs), light rail, fast rail, car share, cable cars, e-cars, maglev, moving platforms and the latest sensation, driverless taxis from Google. For each of these there are nine or more phone apps, intended to seamlessly integrate the whole suite of machines into our lives. Where is Dieter Rams when you need him?

41
'Dieter Rams: Ten Principles for Good Design'. Available online: https://www.vitsoe.com/rw/about/good-design, accessed 16 July 2014.

42
'Beach Pneumatic Transit'. Available online: http://www.nycsubway.org/wiki/Beach_Pneumatic_Transit, accessed 16 July 2014.

43
Leo Marx, *The Machine in the Garden: Technology and the Pastoral Ideal in America* (New York: Oxford University Press, 1964).

44
David Block-Schachter,
'The Myth of the Single
Mode Man: How the
Mobility Pass Better Meets
Actual Travel Demand',
MA Thesis (Cambrige, MA:
Massachusetts Institute of
Technology, 2009).

45
So much has been written
about car manufactures'
role in the demise of
streetcars in the U.S.,
by some who call it a
conspiracy and others
who call the story a myth,
that Robert Post treats the
debate with the serious-
ness it receives in the 1988
movie *Who Framed Roger
Rabbit* that parodies those
events. Robert C. Post,
*Urban Mass Transit: The
Life Story of a Technology*
(Westport: Greenwood
Press, 2007), 155. His final
word is that streetcars
were a victim of their own
success by creating the
conditions of sprawling
cities for cars to later
take over.

46
Taras Grescoe, *Strap-
hanger: Saving Our Cities
and Ourselves from the
Automobile* (New York:
Times Books, 2012).

We can avoid convolution in the design of small things. Why not in the design of the city? It can't be too hard. Let us start by breaking the problem down to a few logical propositions.

Through the exercise of pure reason we can deduce the potential of a city without all these accessories – or at least with a tight ration of them, hidden away and not influencing planning decisions. Then, through empirical observation of places like Copenhagen in the 1920s, or todays pedestrianized town centres, for example in northern Italy, we can learn by our eyes how cycling and walking harmonize on a free plane. Know- ing the speed of a bike (>15 kph) and the size of most cities (<15-km wide), we realise that it isn't distance that makes cycling slow, but all the gadgets we've put in its way, most notably cars and their traffic signals. We have all the knowledge we need to embark on the design of a truly elegant model for city planning, stripped back to basics, with the basics accentuated to optimize elegant means – like walking and cycling – of connecting buildings one to another. The disabled won't be forgotten, nor will logistics, only the makers of convoluted machines.

## Cycling and Public Transport: Take Away Cars and it's a Zero Sum Game

In a sense this line of questioning is a replay of the 1930s when visionary architects imagined cities where everyone drove, only this time we're envisioning cities where the dominant mode of transport is cycling. Alarm bells are probably ringing. Is this going to pan out like a utopian trea- tise for a singular idea that will never be able to be implemented or that would unleash unimaginable consequences if by some miracle it could be – presumably at the hands of a dictator? Of concern too is the very idea of monomodality, which in this age of car-centric cities has come to be viewed as inherently suspect.[44] Surely there are echoes as well of the kinds of corrupt dealings, like the 'streetcar conspiracy',[45] that took place the last time one transport technology was pushed upon every citizen.

Those are just the alarm bells for those of us with an interest in the history of spatial politics. The main reservation about a bike-centric city is obvious even to the unlearned: not every person among us can ride. Due to neurological or physical impairments, or simply because they have the wrong disposition, some people will never be able to participate in bicycle transport, not even on trikes. Meanwhile, any among us could find ourselves too sick to cycle on a day that we needed to travel.

We should not be concerned about people in this category with the money to use a taxi. In a purpose-built bicycle city that has been densely developed on flat lands and that has no cars or traffic lights, pedicabs would be faster and cheaper than the taxis we have at the moment. We all know the frustration of watching the meter tick over while our motorized taxi sits stuck in one of these jams that large vehi- cles bring on each another.

Our concern should be for those who can't pedal or afford taxis. We should spare a thought too for people like Taras Grescoe, the author of *Straphanger*, who happens to enjoy riding with others.[46] Designing for cycling shouldn't mean we insist that every last person aged eight to eighty *must* cycle, or that everyone with Parkinson's Disease has to learn from the sufferer who made the world news by riding a bike even though his legs were too frozen to walk,[47] or that the blind can ride tandems or else learn to use new sonar equipment that will allow them to see the way bats do.[48] There will always be people who reasonably require public transport. Where would bike-city vision leave them?

There is no sugar coating this. Trains would not run every 5 or 10 minutes in a purpose-built bicycle city the way they do in New York. Once a city is freed up for people to travel by bike, the bike is what most people will choose.

Survey data gathered by the Dutch Ministry of Transport in 2009 found seven in ten Dutch people derive joy from bicycle transport.[49] Contrastingly, only one in ten derive joy from public transport. The same survey revealed what its apologists can never admit, that public transport has the highest associations with feelings of fear, anger, sadness and aversion – and that is in a country where public transport is clean and mainstream, not just a safety net for the wretched.

Imagine if the tables were turned and Dutch cities were planned around cycling, then transit was added. At the moment it's the other way around. Since a purpose-built bicycling city would optimize the mode that already brings joy, it might have an even greater percentage of people on bikes than Dallas-Fort Worth has people in cars. We know where that would leave public transport: so poorly patronized that it would need subsidies just to survive.

Many of us living in cities where an 80 to 90 per cent car modal share means buses only run every hour would see nothing wrong with bikes trading places with cars in that scenario. Public transport would flounder, as it has anyway, but hey, the car modal share would be 2 per cent!

It's a different matter for cities like New York, London, Paris and Amsterdam. There, an 80 or 90 per cent bike modal share would seriously wound public transport.

But wouldn't public transport have been wounded in those cities already if the same kind of money had been spent on bike infrastructure as they have spent on their metros? For what it has paid on rail and light rail, Amsterdam could have put cars and trucks underground and put a glass roofs over every person's head on a bike. In other words, it could have given cyclists the kind of protected smooth passage that patrons of public transport enjoy inside carriages.

It seems like a strange thing to say, but conditions for cycling in Amsterdam are just bad enough to make public transport better than it would otherwise be, with a 20 per cent share of all trips[50] (46 per cent in one of its boroughs)[51] and services that run every 6 to 12 minutes.[52] The reason twice as many people are using public transport in Amsterdam than the preference survey suggests, is the other two options haven't been planned for. Driving wasn't planned for in inner boroughs meaning parking costs fortunes and the most joy-inducing option, cycling, has not been made as easy as it would need to be for everyone in Amsterdam

**47**
'Man with Parkinson's Disease Rides a Bike', *The Sydney Morning Herald* (29 November 2012). Available online: http://media.smh.com.au/news/world-news/man-with-parkinsons-disease-rides-a-bike-3849008.html, accessed 14 August 2014.

**48**
See: 'Ultrasound Device 'Gives Blind People Ability to Cycle Safely', *The Telegraph* (30 September 2013). Available online: http://www.telegraph.co.uk/technology/news/10344288/Ultrasound-device-gives-blind-people-ability-to-cycle-safely.html, accessed 14 August 2014.

**49**
Knowledge Institute Mobility (2007) as sited in: Ministerie van Verkeer en Waterstaat 'Cycling in the Netherlands' (2009). Available online: http://www.fietsberaad.nl/library/repository/bestanden/Cyclingin-theNetherlands2009.pdf, accessed 15 August 1013.

**50**
Mode share data obtained from European Platform on Mobility Management (EPOMM) modal split tool, available online: http://www.epomm.eu/tems/search_city.phtml, accessed 8 April 2015.

**51**
www.amsterdam.nl/bereikbaarheid/thermometer.

**52**
See: 'Tram Travel in Amsterdam', available online: http://www.amsterdamtips.com/tips/amsterdam-trams.php, accessed 18 August 2014.

Pedal powered taxi

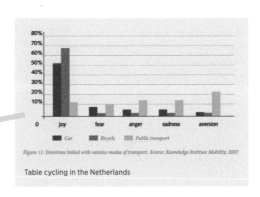

Figure 11: Emotions linked with varoius modes of transport. Source: Knowledge Institute Mobility, 2007

Table cycling in the Netherlands

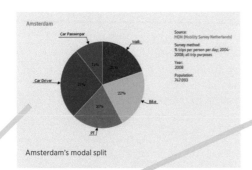

Amsterdam's modal split

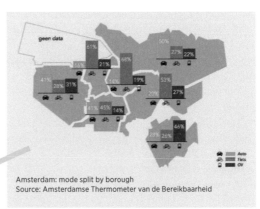

Amsterdam: mode split by borough
Source: Amsterdamse Thermometer van de Bereikbaarheid

Amsterdam tram

Paris Velib bike share

to able to do it. Not everyone has the smarts to join the bike rush hour alongside mopeds and scorchers, with a steampunk bike chain weighing them down as their only insurance against thieves with bolt cutters. Cycling is just tough enough to keep the trams full.

Patronage of public transport is further buoyed by Amsterdam's other significant population, its tourists, who don't have the same easy access to share bikes as tourists in Paris. Bike sharing Vélib' stations are everywhere in Paris and accessible 24/7 for anyone holding a credit card. By contrast there are only 5 MacBike stations in Amsterdam, open from 9:00 AM to 5:45 PM, renting bikes in three-hour blocks.[53]

What does this mean? It means up to half of the people on public transport in Amsterdam are there under sufferance. Even more would be cycling if money were spent to make it as comfortable as sitting aboard a tram.

That's an unfashionable reading, for sure. We are meant to say how great it is for the blind and those like them who can't ride a bike, and for the Millennials who spend their commutes glued to their Facebooks, that public transport in Amsterdam has upwards of 100,000 patrons per day. We're not meant to say that this number might lose a zero if cycling became a lot easier.

To be clear, the thrust of this discussion is not to hurt public transport so that cycling might thrive. The aim is to maximize the mode of maximum benefit and with maximum potential, and that's cycling. It is more than possible that doing so will open the way for new concepts in public transport that will no longer be constrained by a far worse hegemony. Still, it needs to be acknowledged that non-timetabled, high-volume public transport could be an early casualty if a red carpet were rolled out for cycling. A purpose-built bicycling city could leave those who can't possibly cycle at the mercy of the state to subsidize alternatives for them. Some people, in some contexts, might lose. The reality is they are outnumbered 50-to-one by another category of people who are going to die early unless bicycling cities come to the rescue: the obese.

Rates of obesity and chronic disease related to inactivity in the course of our days, are in the order of 20 to 60 per cent, depending on what study you read. Having to wait for the bus is a bummer, but obesity is a first-world disaster. And frequent public transport, where it exists, is doing very little to change that.

The polite fiction of our era, that architects and urban designers have been all too willing to buy into, is that walking a few hundred metres a day between transit hubs and buildings is a good dose of movement to maintain people's health. It isn't that simple. Researchers in the Department of Nutrition at the Harvard School of Public Health checked up on over 18,000 middle-aged women whose weights and activity habits they knew from another study 16 years prior.[54] Their general finding was that, once a person has gained weight, they tend to be unable to lose it if all they are doing is walking. By contrast cycling was found to be helping the slim stay slim, and the overweight lose some, even if they were only cycling for a very short time every day.

What is the difference? It is that too few people are able to walk

[53] http://www.macbike. nl/photo-gallery/ pedalbrake/. Accessed 9 April 2015.

[54] Lusk et al., 'Bicycle Riding, Walking and Weight Gain in Premenopausal Women' *Archives of Internal Medicine*, Vol. 170 (2010) No. 12, 1050-1056. Available online: http://archinte. jamanetwork.com/article. aspx?articleid=416094.

55
This is an argument Dr Anne Lusk of the Harvard School of Public Health has explained in numerous public lectures.

56
For MET scores for walking and cycling see: Ainsworth et al., 'Compendium of Physical Activities: An Update of Activity Codes and MET Intensities', Medicine & Science in Sports & Exercise, Vol. 32 (September 2000) No. 9, 498-504. See also: 'Corrected METs', available online: https://sites.google.com/site/compendiumofphysicalactivities/corrected-mets, accessed 15 August 2014.

briskly enough to really raise their metabolisms. Joint pains that naturally increase with ageing, as well as the excess weight they may already be carrying, makes brisk walking uncomfortable for too many people. All this means walking cannot be counted on as a strategy in environmental design to control obesity and consequences of it like diabetes and hypertension. Bicycling can be. On upright bikes, with their weight relieved from their hips by their saddles, even people with joint pains or excess weight can participate in an activity that cannot help but raise their metabolism into the weight-burning range.[55]

Cycling helps control weight because it raises our metabolic equivalent of task (MET) by on average eight times – compared to a base rate of one while we are resting.[56] The only other activity that speeds our metabolisms like cycling is walking upstairs, which few of us are likely to do for any duration. Casual walking only has an average MET score of three.

What do those numbers mean if we relate them to transport? They tell us that a person will burn four times more calories by riding their bike for half an hour to work, than they would burn if they split that half-hour into 15 minutes of walking and 15 minutes on the tram doing nothing.

If a bicycle city is sounding like some kind of pill, it is worth remembering that pills don't have to be bitter. Think of a bike city as one of those vitamin-C pills that your kids would eat all at once if you let them. There might be an acidic sting somewhere below, but it is masked by a nice mix of sweeteners. One thing that would make a bike city sweet is the time it would free up by making small errands far more efficient, and fun.

# From a
# City for Horses
# to a
# City for Cyclists

# proposition 2

# Copenhagen

Looking along the elevated train line that serves Ørestad

Door-to-door trips from Ørestad to many addresses in the city can be faster by bike than by train. So let's imagine a housing development designed to leave and return to by bike, rather than by car or on foot.

Copenhagen brands itself as a 'city of cyclists', but has no building stock to reflect this. The centre has buildings designed in the age of the horse and the suburbs have houses to drive to, while designers of redevelopment districts assume that people would rather take trains to the city. In other words, their bicycle planning stops at the curb.

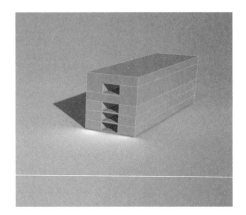

The conceptual starting point is a conventional 'slab block' with double-loaded interior corridors. Lower levels have small single-aspect apartments facing East or West to capture sun daily, even in Winter. Large bayonet apartments on the upper three levels make efficient use of the corridor.

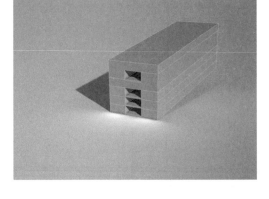

The slab block is tilted by 3 degrees (1 in 20) so the corridors are now ramps suited for not only for bikes but wheelchairs as well and the apartments are staggered.

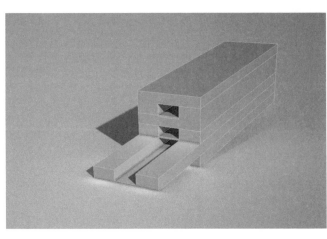

The first floor is extended ('slipped') until the ramped corridor reaches the ground.

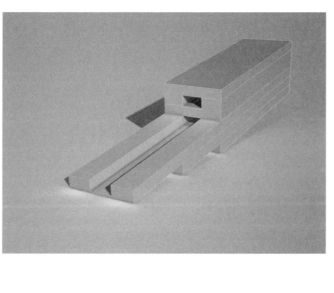

Ditto for floor level two.

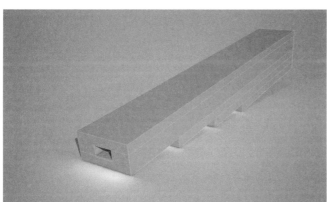

And the same again for the bayonet levels – with one slight addition:

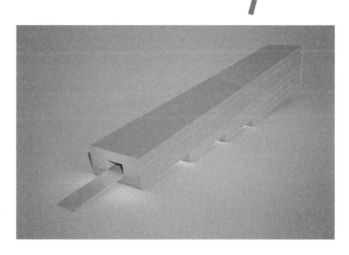

their corridor needs to extend a bit further.

## There is no faster way of coming and going!

A conventional slab block (left) shortens the walking distance to lifts. Also lifts are used to go up and down. What we call a 'slip-block' (right) encourages people to leave on their bikes by giving them gravity assistance from the moment they wheel out of their doors. Since they would only be used (by some) to go up, lifts are provided at the ends of blocks only. Typically, one large lift can serve a whole building.

**Pedestrian paths at the edge of the ramped access-corridors are textured to deter cyclists, while the bike path at the centre is cambered to deter walkers. Visitor bike parking protects each from the other.**

Even the smallest apartments have a bike space within the secure confines of the dwelling, placed to intercept residents as they leave home.

The number of indoor bike parking spaces matches the anticipated number of beds. You're looking at 'start of trip' bike parking facilities, not in a basement, not on the street, but at the point from which trips really start: inside of the home.

Here is a plan of a full-width bayonet flat on the top level (the level with bike parking opening off of the corridor is one floor below).

Every apartment has sunlight and a view over a raised pedestrian concourse spanning a sunken bike-transport layer.

Users of skate parks naturally congregate on the crests

The ground plane treatment is inspired by the BMX park, where riders speed across channels and come to a stop on the crests, all without braking and with minimal pedalling effort.

Here we are looking up from the bicycling channel to a ground level retail location. Commercial tenancies occur every 60 meters and correspond to the bases of the ramped access corridors.

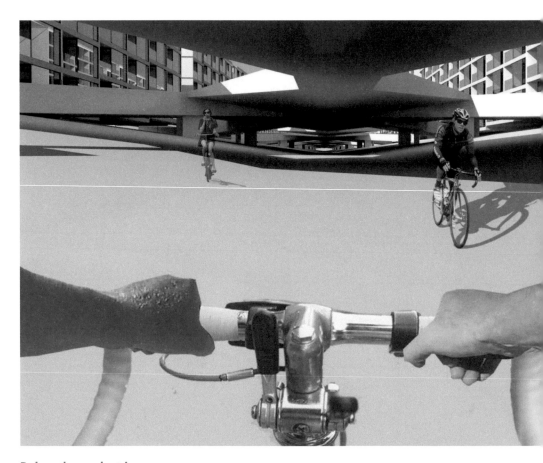

Below the pedestrian concourses riders are protected from rain and have been given gravity assistance to get up to speed upon entry …

while on the concourse, pedestrians and slow riders are protected from commuters speeding below.

As the scheme is meant to be received only as a stark proposition, and catalyst for further debate, the blocks are shown in a rack, oriented to maximise sun penetration.

The wedged-shape of the slip block makes it possible to give most residents views to the city or country over the low ends of neighbouring blocks.

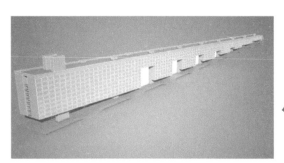

Holes occur above retail hubs at the start of each ramped corridor leading inside to the flats.

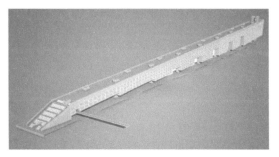

Gentle stair runs with wheel-channels at the ends of the blocks provide access to sloped roof-top recreation areas: sites for ski slopes or mountain bike flow trails.

Low level apartments have filtered views through holes left in each block.

What has not been shown are the many ways this concept could be softened, especially at the ground level. The aim with the *Unite d' Bicycle Nation* is to highlight just how different housing might be if cycling were central to design thinking. In Copenhagen it is still being treated as an add-on, or supplement, to developments that teleologically trace to powered modes of urban transport.

While the two older billy goats packed up the tent,
The youngest one said, "Cheerio!"
He began to trot over the rickety bridge
Just as fast as his two feet would go.

But he had

When
And
And

chapter 2

# How Should We Think About Bicycling Cities?

1930s Bakfiets

Street graffiti

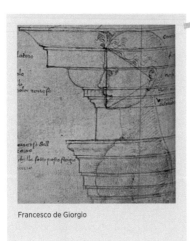

Francesco de Giorgio

Cargo trike

## Purpose-Building for Bikes

Earlier we considered convolution and simplicity at the scale of the city. Let us now narrow our gaze to a non-convoluted machine, the two-wheeled box bike, also known as a Long John, cargo bike or *bakfiets*. They were first used in the 1930s in Denmark and the Netherlands as tradesmen's delivery bikes and have enjoyed a huge wave of new interest since Maarten van Andel rediscovered the design and put it back into production.

Why do their owners love them so much? Dieter Rams has our answer: they are less, but better. They are like a car in having an operator, cargo, main structure and seats. They don't have an engine, though, and this makes them better. They put the operator's own body to work as an engine, increasing the owner's health and wellbeing and giving them less dead weight to manoeuvre and park. Stencil campaigners have illustrated this point.

The box bike has been a tremendous boon for parents in bike friend-ly cities. It has already led to redesigned bike racks.[1] Humble beginnings! This simple device deserves to have whole cities purpose built for it. Corridor widths could be welded to its dimensions the way Renaissance architecture was welded to the proportions of the human body.[2]

Let us not forget that a far less impressive vehicle, the car (a kind of lawnmower disguised with upholstery) has had freeways, suburbs and buildings you can drive-through and drive-into, built especially for it. That was during the first machine age. Now that we're a little more reticent about energy-hungry machines invading our lives, it would make sense to at least try to imagine a city designed around box bikes and bicycling generally.

Let us suppose it did happen. Let's say some conception of a city designed around the box bike was to inspire bicycle-focused greenfield or brownfield redevelopment, or even whole new bike-focused cities. Quite aside from the societal dividends (fewer emissions, fewer road deaths, fewer people with diabetes), there is a real possibility that a purpose-built city for bikes would better satisfy the individual's own selfish aims than a city for cars would. If you think about it, there would not be the same limitations in a purpose-built city for bikes when it comes to penetrating buildings with the vehicles that we use to move between them. Cars are enormous. They can barely penetrate the streets of dense districts, let alone go inside buildings. Bikes can go anywhere.

Even if cars could be made narrow and clean enough to come inside with us, their artificial means of propulsion would always make them too clumsy. Moving with motors is like trying to draw with computers rather than pencils. Actions do not proceed straight from the body and mind but are translated through motors and their controls.

You would never let someone drive into a supermarket and load their car like a trolley, then drive all the way back to their kitchen to unload it directly into their pantry. Display shelves would be toppled and somebody's child would be backed over. However, with a little tweaking of supermarket design, and apartment design, it is possible to imagine

1
See: *The Copenhagenize Bar*. Available online: http://copenhagenize. eu/portfolio/port01.html, accessed 26 July 2014.

2
Rudolf Wittkower describes Renaissance architecture being welded to the proportions of the body. See: Rudolf Wittkower, *Architectural Principles in the Age of Humanism*, (London: Tiranti, 1952).

3
Gerd-Helge Vogel, 'Mobility: The Fourth Dimension in the Fine Arts and Architecture', *Contemporary Aesthetics*, Special Vol. (2005), No. 1.

4
William Gilpin, *Observations on the River Wye: Observations on the River Wye, and Several Parts of South Wales, &c. Relative Chiefly to Picturesque Beauty; Made in the Summer of the Year 1770* (London: 1782). Available online: https://archive.org/details/observationsonr00gilpgoog, accessed 13 March 2015.

5
Ebenezer Howard, *Garden Cities of To-morrow* (London: Swan Sonnenschein & Co., 1902).

that errand being done with a non-motorised box bike. It may just need retractable casters.

A century ago, when Modernists were imagining a future city for cars, they started by asking what design implications grew naturally from the limitations and strengths of their favoured machine. The car's ability to shrink space suggested solutions that were all about spreading out – Frank Lloyd Wright's Broadacre City for instance. The car's poor turning radius gave rise to Euclidian curves such as the cloverleaf intersections that so fascinated Le Corbusier and that he inscribed into the plan of his Villa Savoye.
 A number of defining things can be said about cycling that have implications for a bicycling architecture. Cyclists can traverse cambered surfaces that would hurt peoples' ankles if they were walking. They can squeeze through gaps that powered vehicles cannot. Bikes are safe enough and clean enough to be ridden indoors. They provide the rider with a leaning view of the world when they turn, a view that rushes by quickly when they are heading downhill and a view that adds detail when they lose speed on an incline. Where the car's limitation is its poor turning radius, the bike's limitation is the lack of shelter it gives riders from the sun and the rain. Each of these attributes gives us a hint as to how a bicycle urbanism would differ from urbanisms built around driving, or indeed any mode other than cycling.

A lot of the diversity we find among building types and urban patterns is a factor of the diverse ways we as humans can move. We can understand this by recognizing that, to even exist as an art, architecture relies on us moving, just as literature relies on us reading or paintings require us to shine a light on them. According to Gerd-Helge Vogel, our progression from a species that largely stays put to one that is mobile has led to mobility becoming architecture's fourth, and hidden, dimension.[3]
 So consider these examples: how walking inspired porticoes, ambulatories – virtually everything; how boating didn't just give us passenger terminals, but Venice, William Gilpin's key text on the picturesque that starts with a riverboat trip[4] and the twentieth-century fashion of buildings resembling ocean liners; how flying has given us airports; how train travel gave us George Gilbert Scott's St Pancras station and comes in for repeated mention throughout Ebenezer Howard's *Garden Cities of To-morrow*;[5] and how driving was behind a raft of new building types, plus the proliferation of cottages in suburban and urban locations.
 The all-too-humble bicycle has no such legacy. How many buildings try to capture the essence of two-wheeled human powered movement? The velodrome? BIG's Danish Pavilion at the Shanghai Expo in 2010? There really aren't many.

It is laudable that the cities of Houten and Milton Keynes had bike routes planned from the start, but that hardly makes these examples of bicycle urbanism. In both cases far-weightier design constraints stemmed from the decision to build access for cars.
 It is encouraging too that an architectural idiom has appeared in new Dutch and Danish architecture: the giant awning protecting parked

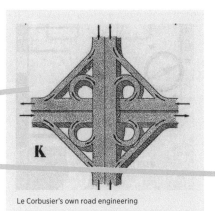

Le Corbusier's own road engineering

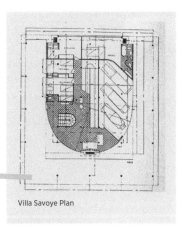

Villa Savoye Plan

Velodrome

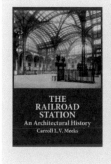

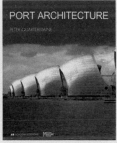

Danish Pavilion

Berlin Velodrome

6
Jeff Olson highlights the
injustice of cyclists being
punished for doing good.
See: Jeff Olson, *The Third
Mode: Towards a Green
Society* (2012).

bikes near the door. If we want to find anything more, though, we'll be scratching for examples of architects doing as little as possible just to appease nagging cyclists, who must be appeased because we do good.[6] But there's a nagging sense architects secretly loath people cycling for turning the entrance ways of their buildings into chaotic piles of bent steel. Many would probably prefer their buildings be photographed at the moment a truck arrived to collect garbage than when hundreds of bikes were piled near the entrance.

Attitudes would be turned on their heads if architects could muster some general excitement about cycling to match the excitement for driving shown by pioneers of the modernist style: Antonio Sant'Elia, Harvey Wiley Corbett, Le Corbusier, Frank Lloyd Wright, Buckminster Fuller, etcetera. Better still, they might conjure that sense of delight they had as a child when they realized the grown-up teaching them to ride had just let go of their saddle and for the first time in their life they were cycling. If we could have that moment again, now that we are designers, how would we mould the ground stretched before us? How would we shape our buildings and cities?

Following are five defining characteristics of built space that speak to the sensation of cycling:
1. the ground plane is cambered in ways that might hurt our ankles if we were walking, but which feels wonderful under our tires – we would thus find very few people walking in front of us on this surface;
2. related to the first point, undulations help us speed up and slow down without braking or pedalling harder;
3. the space we are in is quarantined from faster vehicles;
4. we can find shelter if we need to get out of the sun or the rain;
5. everything is further apart than if it were designed for our speed before we could ride and thus had to walk.

Empiricists, who need to relate every new thought to something they have experienced with their senses, would struggle to follow this. 'Where are these five characteristics in the Netherlands or Denmark?' they might be asking. That is the empiricism's shortcoming.

We need on occasion to be of rationalistic mindset. Rationalists throughout history like René Descartes and Plato have maintained that observable models can be a barrier to people using pure reason. From a rationalistic standpoint our eyes should not be so seduced by what we see in Amsterdam or Copenhagen that our minds can't freely imagine a district built especially for cycling. Empiricists need constant reminding that old cities were built for walking and horses. The bicycles came much later.

The Royal Danish Playhouse

Faculty of Science University of Utrecht

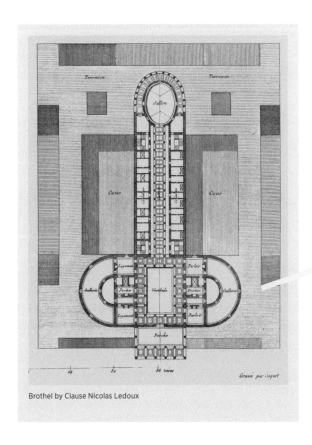

Brothel by Clause Nicolas Ledoux

## Epistemology and Building-Type Classifications

7
Anthony Vidler, 'The Idea of Type: The Transformation of an Academic Idea 1750-1830' (1977), in: K. Michael Hays (Ed.), The Oppositions Reader (New York: Princeton Architectural Press, 1998), 437-459.

8
Alan Colquhoun, 'Typology and Design Method' (1967), in: Kate Nesbitt (Ed.), Theorizing a New Agenda for Architecture. An Anthology of Architectural Theory 1965-1995 (New York: Princeton Architectural Press, 1996), 248. First printed in: Essays in Architectural Criticism. Modern Architecture and Historical Change (Cambridge, MA: MIT Press, 1981).

9
It has been said by Alfred North Whitehead that the whole 'European philosophical tradition . . . consists of a series of footnotes to Plato'. See: Alfred North Whitehead, Process and Reality (New York: Free Press, 1979), 39.

10
See: Sylvia Lavin, Quatremère de Quincy and the Invention of a Modern Language of Architecture (Cambridge, MA: The MIT Press, 1992).

11
Giulio Carlo Argan, 'On the Typology of Architecture' (1963), in: Kate Nesbitt (Ed.), Theorizing a New Agenda for Architecture. An Anthology of Architectural Theory 1965-1995 (New York: Princeton Architectural Press, 1996), 240-247.

12
Steven Fleming, The Bed Maker's Model: A Thematic Study of Louis I. Kahn's 1961 Article 'Form and Design' in Terms of Plato's Theory of Forms as Treated in The Republic (Saarbrücken: VDM Verlag, 2009).

13
Cassette recording, 'The Scope of Architecture at The Cooper Union Hall, 1-20-60', Louis I. Kahn Collection, University of Pennsylvania and Pennsylvania Historical and Museum Commission.

Here is a syllogism:

Major premise: we want everyone cycling! That is because cycling performs three miracles at the same time: 1) reducing door-to-door travel times in dense cities (especially if the ground plane can be cleared of most cars and their traffic lights can be removed); 2) vaccinating populations against chronic disease; 3) reducing greenhouse emissions.

Minor premise: new urban districts continue to be built. Whether through sprawling, thickening, backfilling or building new cities from scratch, there are always new streets and private lots being made.

Inference: we need to conceptualize new ways of developing cities so they encourage people to choose cycling over all other modes.

Experts in other fields might see different inferences, like removing financial incentives to drive or use public transport, or introducing laws to make drivers slow down. However, any inferences for us as designers must relate to the production of built environments.

Historically, when new circumstances have occasioned a need for new building types, the most common response has been to take a known type and adapt it. The adaptation of the basilica form to make the first churches in Rome is one good example.

The idea of starting from scratch when inventing particular plan forms to match particular functions arose during the Enlightenment when, for example, Jeremy Bentham invented the Panopticon prison and Claude Nicolas Ledoux pioneered the notion of *architecture parlante*, or 'speaking architecture'. Here was his plan for a brothel.

When it comes to new building types, architectural inventiveness seems to rise in proportion to social upheaval. With the shift to socialism in Russia, architects abruptly stopped building axially-symmetrical palaces and invented new building types like the 'social condenser', a building where the arrangement of spaces for sleeping, eating and childcare would make it impossible to know whose children were whose. Moisei Ginzburg's and Ignatii Milinis's 1928 Narkomfin Building is the most famous example, with an arrangement of spaces designed to destroy the institution of inherited wealth.

Most of what has been written about theories of types in architecture, for example by Anthony Vidler[7] and Alan Colquhoun,[8] can be summarized as footnotes to Plato.[9] Irrespective of whether they agree with Plato, like Quatremère de Quincy,[10] or disagree like Giulio Carlo Argan,[11] they take Plato's theory of Forms, or Ideas, as their main point of reference. My own doctoral project unearthed one of the most explicit echoes of Plato's theory by an architect in modern times.[12] That was by the architect Louis Kahn, who told a Cooper Union audience in 1960 that an architect needs to be like Socrates when contemplating the type/Idea/Form or 'form' that should be the model for every school.[13]

While intellectually uneasy to swallow in our post-Enlightenment age, it is fascinating all the same to imagine a transcendent recipe for every classifiable type of building that might ever come into existence. Imagine, for example, that the ideal teleportation centre already exists,

Narkomfin Building

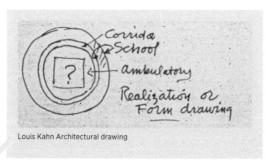

Louis Kahn Architectural drawing

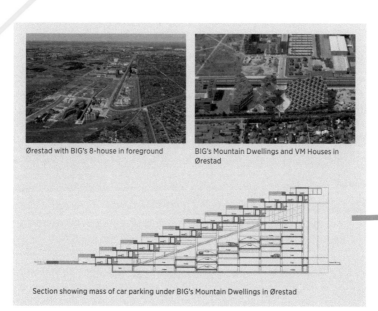

Ørestad with BIG's 8-house in foreground

BIG's Mountain Dwellings and VM Houses in Ørestad

Section showing mass of car parking under BIG's Mountain Dwellings in Ørestad

14
For a commentary on Plato that casts doubt on the assumption that he believed his own speculations see: John Herman Randall, Jr., *Plato: Dramatist of the Life of Reason* (New York: Columbia University Press, 1970).

15
Anthony Vidler, 'The Third Typology', *Oppositions*, No. 7 (1976), 1-4.

not in material form, but as an Idea. Or imagine that 'The Hospital for Raising the Dead' might exist as an Idea, just waiting for the day when we have the technology to bring back the dead and we suddenly need buildings to cope with the unforeseen chaos. Would it need waiting rooms for the great-great-great-grandchildren?

We can leave it to future generations of architects to grapple with the optimal building type for exhuming the dead. The task facing our generation is realizing (or moreover *inventing*) the optimal forms needed to make non-congested, non-obesogenic and non-polluting new cities. Fast, healthy and green: we could talk about approaches that might win us two, or we could talk about cycling that will win us all three.

If we think philosophically about the problem of inventing new building types and public-space principles that encourage the greatest possible use of the bike, we realize that neither Amsterdam or Copenhagen are any better suited as models than the basilica was a great model for churches. All that can be said for those cities is they have been nicely adapted for cycling, having first been designed for walking and horses. The question here, though, is not how to adapt cities for bikes. Cities have so much real growth, on vacant land, projected for them that we can ask questions about the optimal, purpose-built city for bikes. If this were a dialogue by Plato, we would be italicizing the term 'The Bicycle City Itself' to make it clear we are discussing a Platonic Form or Idea. However, we don't have to believe that transcendent ideals are out there in the Form-realm or heaven to approach this as a question. We can in fact be like Plato, who simply hypothesized about the existence of Forms, or Ideas, as a first step toward thinking more clearly.[14]

## Ørestad: Why We Need an Idea

Why do we need to imagine a purpose-built bicycling city? It is not so we can bulldoze old city centres. The reason we need a new model of urban development, conceived upon a bicycle mobility platform, is so we can stop the proliferation of brand new urban districts with racetrack-style curbs and basement car parking.

These aren't only being built in developing countries like China and India. Disappointingly, even Copenhagen has done it. The new district of Ørestad, just 15 minutes by bike from a CBD that boasts having more bike trips than all other modes put together, is being built over enormous garages and has roads designed to go fast on.

Like brownfield redevelopment districts in all post-industrial cities, Ørestad began life with a master plan showing buildings turned outward to the street. Anyone who can remember architectural journals of the 1970s or 1980s would not be surprised by that master plan.

Hardly an edition of the key architectural journal of that time, *Oppositions*, passed without an article on some aspect of the European old town, teased out and presented as a principle that ought to be replicated in redevelopment districts. As early as 1976 Anthony Vidler was saying the traditional European city had replaced the machine as the architect's main inspiration.[15] That set the stage for the 1978 exhibition 'Roma Interrotta' (Rome interrupted) featuring future visions for Rome by architects including James Stirling, Romaldo Giurgola, Robert Venturi, Colin Rowe, Michael Graves, Rob and Léon Krier and Aldo Rossi – all the great names of the time.[16] While each had to project into the future with what they presented, they were also required to pay homage to Giambattista Nolli's 1784 map. Nolli used a figure-ground method of representation that naturally draws attention to the narrow streets and perimeter blocks of Rome. Both were at the forefront of architects' thinking as they strived to make cities legible, with liveable streets and a strong sense of what many at the time referred to as *civitas*.

Looking today at actual redevelopment districts like Ørestad, we cannot say their overblown scale is the result of architects not caring about street life or human scale. The leading thinkers of our discipline were absorbed by these topics right up until the development cycle of the 1990s and 2000s when their ideas had the chance to be built. The question we should really be asking is what on earth has gone wrong that places like Ørestad drifted from the theories that architects had been slaving to perfect in preceding decades?

Part of the answer is that, by the time investor confidence peaked in the early 2000s, developers and financiers weren't interested in boutique in-fill apartment buildings – the basic type that gives historic districts their character. They wanted to do developments that took up a whole block (a.k.a. 'blockbuster' developments). We can understand why. With size comes economy. The cost of lifts, rubbish removal systems, landscaping, prototyping and the even some of the latest energy saving techniques are all proportionally cheaper when you build hundreds of apartments instead of dozens.

These are all plusses to large-scale construction, not only for developers but apartment buyers as well, and potentially even the planet. However, there is one undeniable minus. The greater the sums of money invested the more conservative investors become. The world's pension funds, banks and other financiers resorted to a nervous, retrograde vision during the boom of the early 2000s. It is a vision that is predicated on lots of car parking and roads designed to look more like formula-one race tracks than the kinds of streets our ancestors built in the age of horses and walking.

We have to remember that their retrograde vision is only man made. It blasted into the cultural imagination with the 'Futurama' exhibition at the 1939 New York World's Fair, and was rapidly built in the U.S. after the Second World War from a huge one-time government surplus that President Truman was anxious to spend. It was so successfully branded as 'progress' that it was copied all over the world: ribbons of highways cutting through cities; suburbia spreading over horizons; and every creative means of adding car access and parking.

Nevertheless, this vision is only a human creation. It can be unpicked. We see that, in city centres with street layouts predating the car, cars can be turned away as they reach city limits. Downtowns are being freed up for inhabitants for whom driving means nothing, either because they are poor (as in cities like Bogota) or because they have nowhere to park (as is the case for many in the centre of London).

16
This famous exhibition was on show again in Rome's Maxxi Museum in 2014. See online: http://www.fondazionemaxxi.it/2014/02/22/trabetween-arte-e-architettura/, accessed 26 July 2014.

8-House by BIG

Futurama Exhibition 1939 World's Fair New York

The next frontiers on which the Futurama vision can be debunked are all those places where cities are due to be built or expanded. These are in developing countries and on our own redundant industrial lands. Can we stop these being planned around cars?

We will need to first recognize that there is no hidden force, in nature or heaven, causing car dependent cities to self-replicate. Henri Lefebvre gave us a beautiful phrase, 'The Production of Space', to remind us that the space we inhabit is one we create as a culture.[17] In this space we agree to behave in certain ways – to drive in, to farm on, to be naked or clothed – determined by us. Urban space is like the map and the rules of a video game that no one would pretend was there all along.[18] Somebody made it. The same is true of every new land subdivision, with streets designed to move cars between buildings. Each is a mistake that we as a species need to own up to.

## The Utility and Folly of Utopian Visions

Imagine a mother riding a box bike. She has a shopping list in her pocket and a baby being bounced to sleep. She has just ridden down out of her apartment. In what sort of neighbourhood does she find herself?

For the sake of a more productive discussion let's run with the idea that this is a hypothetical mother. It would thus be a hypothetical neighbourhood awaiting her at ground level. Let's make no bones about this: for the purpose of this discussion she has arrived in a bicycling utopia, an imaginary happy/no place. Should it be her dream to live in a city where she can choose to ride sheltered from of the sun or the rain, then this imaginary place has overhead canopies and vast areas where she can cycle completely indoors. If she dreams of not having to brake to slow down or pedal to get herself going, then the intersections and activity nodes in this bicycling utopia would be raised on slight mounds while express routes would follow deep channels. If she would be frightened by cyclists whizzing around her while she was walking or riding at walking pace, then this bicycling utopia would have elevated bridges between the raised activity nodes to provide her with grade separation from the gravity-forced zone lower down.

What a shame we can't speak this way about utopian visions. To planners the word "utopia" is an affront to tenets that they hold dear, for example that bottom-up initiatives are better than projects dropped from above, that piecemeal implementation is better than mass roll-outs and that city growth should be 'organic'. As general rules all these would be fine. It's a problem when hacks recite them as dogmas.

Architects have convinced themselves that utopian visions only make the world worse. Isn't that the story of Pruitt-Igoe? The role of architecture, therefore, is to hold a mirror to a world in decline as Peter Eisenman et. al. taught a generation to do through architectural representation.

The only architects not too savvy to dream of utopias are men above ninety who missed the shift in opinion. Paolo Soleri devoted a lifetime to conceiving and promoting self-contained hyper-dense cities. He died in

17
Henri Lefebvre, *The Production of Space* (Hoboken: Wiley-Blackwell, 1991).

18
Douglas Lain, *The Production Of Space Understood Through Video Games*. Available online: http://thoughtcatalog.com/doug-lain/2011/05/the-production-of-space-understood-through-video-games/, accessed 23 April 2014.

19
Aaron Betsky, *Violated Perfection: Architecture and the Fragmentation of the Modern* (New York: Rizzoli, 1990).

20
Karsten Harries, *The Ethical Function of Architecture* (Cambridge, MA: The MIT Press, 1998).

21
Franco Borsi, *Architecture and Utopia* (Paris: Editions Hazan, 1997).

22
Karl Popper, *The Poverty of Historicism* (Boston: The Beacon Press, 1957).

23
David Gosling and Barry Maitland, *Concepts of Urban Design* (London: Academy Editions, 1984).

24
Lewis Mumford, *The Story of Utopias* (New York: Viking Press, 1950), 11.

25
Karl Popper, *The Poverty of Historicism* (Boston: The Beacon Press, 1957).

26
Christopher Alexander, *The Process of Creating Life: Nature of Order, Book 2: An Essay on the Art of Building and the Nature of the Universe* (Berkeley: Center for Environmental Structure, 2006).

2013 at age 93. Tragically, 97 per cent of his prototype city, Arcosanti, was still incomplete. But as Aaron Betsky has said, Arcosanti's central idea of autonomous 'self-building' was a farce from the start, with the community depending on the sale of handcrafts to tourists for cash.[19]

Some cruel people laugh at Soleri. Many more laugh at Jacque Fresco. This plucky centenarian and die-hard believer in Buckminster Fuller's wildest ideas has spent a lifetime filming miniature models in the belief that his Venus Project is paving the way for a future of infinite abundance when all work is done by machines.

These are just goofy-faced totems. Behind them is an actual demon that we truly fear. When serious architectural writers mention utopias they point to Albert Speer's plan for Berlin,[20] or remind us that when utopias come into being they have a concentration-camp charm.[21]

This association between utopianism and despotism can be traced to Karl Popper, the famous philosopher of science. In *The Poverty of Historicism* he attacks social engineers (particularly Marxists, who he had previously called pseudoscientists) who try to impose their version of an ideal social order upon everyone under their power.[22] His critique might never have come onto architects' radars except for the fact that a word from our lexicon, utopian, was used to describe those social engineers he despised.

It is due to this confusion that a key book for urban designers by David Gosling and Barry Maitland quotes Popper at length.[23] Popper's preference for organic growth and his dismissal of preconceptions are spelled out and related to urban design. However, Popper's actual focus was not urban design but social engineering. Nevertheless, Gosling and Maitland take all of Popper's complaints about utopian social engineering being 'unscientific, oppressive, [and] unable to learn from its mistakes', and level them squarely at Filarete, Claude Nicolas Ledoux, Ebenezer Howard, Le Corbusier, Buckminster Fuller and by implication anyone whose work has been motivated by a preconceived vision of an ideal city plan.

Quoting Popper again, Gosling and Maitland warn against accepting 'the colossal assumption that we need not question the fundamental benevolence of the planning Utopian engineer.' What they are saying is that people like Soleri and Fresco are to be suspected of malevolent aims, like Hitler or Stalin.

To be fair, Popper's thinking about utopian visions has pollinated urban-design theory in positive ways. Before him the last word on the subject belonged to Lewis Mumford who had rather simplistically argued in 1950 that the only thing wrong with utopian visions is they are not always enacted, putting some visions in the category of utopian fantasies of escape.[24] Popper, by advocating a piecemeal style of social engineering that learns from its mistakes and is 'always on the lookout for the unavoidable unwanted consequences of any reform', makes Mumford look somewhat gung ho.[25] Thanks to Popper's influence architects have become suitably reticent. Consider Christopher Alexander who in *The Nature of Order* argues that city planners can start with an ideal model as a catalyst in the back of their mind, but must accept that the final form of a city will be the result of monitoring, adjustments and tweaking.[26]

visualisation gravity-fed bike lane

Jacque Fresco with Venus Project model

Arconsanti

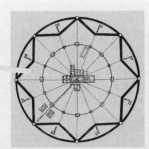

Sforzinda by Filarete

Royal Salt Works - Ledoux

Cloud Nine floating cities by Buckminster Fuller

27
Françoise Choay, *The Rule and the Model: On the Theory of Architecture and Urbanism*, edited by Denise Bratton (Cambridge, MA: The MIT Press, 1997), 7.

28
Thomas More, *Utopia*, translated by Peter Turner (London: Penguin, [1516] 1965). Note too that there are other utopian models dating as least as far back as Plato. See: S. Lang, 'The Ideal City from Plato to Howard', *The Architectural Review*, Vol. 112 (1952) No. 668, 91-101.

29
Françoise Choay, 'On the Disaster of Amnesia. An Interview with Françoise Choay', *Archis*, No. 4 (2003), 26-31. Available online: https://www.academia.edu/1075302/On_the_disaster_of_amnesia._An_interview_with_Francoise_Choay, accessed 22 August 2014.

30
Ibid.

However, that's not exactly Popper's position. His view is that a priori assumptions themselves are the problem. Social engineers should have no preconceived notions of a better or a worse world, just a willingness to tinker, monitor and discuss as they go.

What needs spelling out, a second time, is that Popper was not writing about urban planning. His quarrel was with ideologically driven social engineers, specifically the Marxists and fascists who he equally blamed for having prevented a rise of democratic liberalism in his own homeland of Austria, a situation that would lead to his exile.

Urban planners deserve a unique dispensation to speak in utopian strains. Even Gosling and Maitland admit this. After explaining all Popper's concerns they go on to say that the value of utopian visions, in urban design, is they are catalytic – never mind the handful of fools who treat them as prescriptions. Utopian visions bring clarity to real world debates, Gosling and Maitland maintained, 'by postulating alternative hypotheses in a pure and crystalline form'.

One of the key texts on utopian thinking, insofar as the discipline of urban design is concerned, is Françoise Choay's *The Rule and the Model*.[27] It is a book about what Choay calls an 'audacious' enterprise, called urbanism, that arose to shape cities through deliberate planning rather than just leaving matters to chance. Starting in the sixteenth century this new discipline was made possible because Leon Battista Alberti had introduced the idea of a 'rule' in his ten books, and because Thomas More had introduced the idea of a 'model' in his 1516 novel *Utopia*.[28] Urbanism arose in the dialectical space between models pulling on planner's minds from one side and rules pulling on their minds from the other.

While models and rules are treated as two sides of the one coin in her book, a few years after *The Rule and the Model* was translated into English Choay gave an interview in which she made it clear which side of that coin she favoured. Rules are flexible. Models are static. Rules can be creatively reinterpreted for different places and times. Models and contexts are always at odds. She contrasts 'the limitations of More's model, which allows no room for individual expression, with Alberti's idea of a virtually unlimited deployment of individual expression'.[29]

What she still doesn't say, though, is that urbanism can exist without utopian models. One undeniable reason is utopian models are so stirring that no one, having once been exposed, can shut them out of their minds – or as Choay writes:

> The reason why I nevertheless hold that the utopia, as a literary genre, is entirely qualified to be considered an instaurational text [like a treatise] is it is organically connected with the urban theories it preceded, having stamped upon their form its indelible imprint.[30]

What would today's planners and architects make of Choay's claim? Surely their urban theories aren't indelibly stamped by past utopian models? The planners are busy being bottom-up, piecemeal and organic. The architects are holding a mirror to a world in decline. Their theories can't be utopian. Can they?

If we think about transport, it is easy to see how they are. Insofar as transport is concerned, today's urban theories have utopian pedigrees dating as far back as the turn of the last century.

Take the principle of consolidating development within walking distance of train stations, but otherwise spreading out. This is indelibly stamped by Howard's circular diagram of transit-oriented Garden Cities. Less flatteringly, architects' and planners' permissiveness in the face of ongoing sprawl betrays the indelible stamp of Wright's Broadacre City that he based on the idea that cars would let us each live on an acre and pretend we are framers.

Most embarrassing are today's inner city apartments. Built over batteries of multistorey car parking, and beside roads that look like go-carting circuits, most bear the indelible stamp of the General Motors 'Highways and Horizons' pavilion with its 'Futurama' exhibition.

Thinking back to Popper, we could say each of these three models is an a priori assumption about directions cities can head in. Another way is to think of each as a game with its own rules. You only have to have built your own house to have had first-hand experience in one of these games: Wright's game called Broadacre. You will have asked yourself how the car could be brought in from the road, how close it could be parked to kitchen and the distance in minutes (never mind units of spatial measure-ment) between the house and the nearest roadside supermarket, school, technology park or whatever destinations were important to you.

What is interesting about all three of these games is they can be played simultaneously on the same field – that field being a city. Players of the Broadacre game might spend a lot of time around the outskirts of the field. Players with the rules of the Garden-Cities game on their minds would stick to prescribed pathways that funnel them between the goals and other key points on the field. Players who are inspired by the inner-city apartment towers of Norman Bel Geddes's 1939 'Futurama' would have a place to live near the goals, and a car to go play with their Broadacre friends in the outfield. In other words, actual cities can have superimposed utopian visions. In application those visions all get entan-gled, but as theories they are each crystal clear.

A book that helps us understand cities as fields where multiple games – each pure unto itself – are played all at once, is Italo Calvino's *Invisible Cities*.[31] It is a novel that instead of a plot or character develop-ment has Marco Polo giving descriptions to Kublai Khan of cities he has seen in his travels. In one of Calvino's invisible cities all that can be seen is the plumbing running skyward with no masonry or framing around it; looking up you see all the ladies in their bathrooms and plumbing fixtures discharging over their bath tubs. Another city consists entirely of the cor-ruption one might find in a city – nothing else is described. Another city is nothing but signage and would remind architects of one of their most important books of the past century, *Learning from Las Vegas*.

Irrespective of whether each is to be interpreted as a different view of the one city (some say the book presents more than 50 different ways to see Venice), or whether each is a city in its own right, in a sense they are all like the Broadacre, Garden Cities and Futurama that manage to coexist in so many of the cities we know.

31
Italo Calvino, *Invisible Cities*, translated by William Weaver (San Diego: Harcourt Brace Jovanovich, 1974).

Futurama exhibition

Invisible Cities

Accepting that cities have systems and agendas that all overlap makes those libertarians among us want to protect the dreams of the few from the dreams of the many when the latter start crushing the former. Many people want to live the Broadacre dream. We know they are eating of the future with their fuel consumption,[32] but we would rather live and let live than intervene on their liberty, on one proviso: that their pursuit of their dream does not interfere with others' pursuance of theirs. Let them blacken the sky, but if they park their cars over cycle tracks they deserve to be fined and shamed via social media. Let them fill hospital waiting rooms as they age, just don't let their rat-runs (connector roads) endanger our children when our children are cycling to school. Let them vote for wars over oil, just don't let them drive with abandon on the quiet back streets where we ride our bikes to avoid their arterial roads. Let them pursue their Wrightian-utopian vision, but in ways that don't negate our pursuit of our visions.

Modernism provided more than just an approach to the design of particular buildings. It encompassed a vision for the design of the streets that tie buildings together. As architects we tend to forget that our discipline's backlash against modernism only looked at the first half of that equation. Peter Blake,[33] Brent Brolin[34] and later Tom Wolfe[35] criticized modernist buildings, not modernist street engineering. Everything its chief critic Charles Jencks said about modernism – for example, that it was 'the son of the Enlightenment' and therefore 'an heir to its congenital naiveties'[36] – could just as easily have been said about reengineered streets, but it wasn't. It was the buildings that Jencks said had 'the faults of an age trying to reinvent itself totally on rational grounds', in a way that was as silly as the 'rational design of women's bloomers', but what the engineers were doing to streets with that attitude was far more impactful.

Modernist architecture was hardly as bad as modernist road engineering. The architects produced isolated buildings that people were free to look away from if not to their taste. Proponents of modernist road engineering were trying to stamp out any other kind of environment than the one they envisioned. A variety of uses ranging from milling, cycling, horse riding and what came to be referred to as 'jaywalking' (an allusion to jaybirds/criminals) were being erased to make way for ostensibly two uses: driving petrol-powered machines and walking short distances to where they were parked.

Modernist buildings were hardly that dictatorial. In many cases their complex arrangements of spaces, articulated façades and glass-curtain walls added to the number of ways to imagine the city. Where architects overstepped their jurisdiction was with totalitarian visions, like London's planned network of 'pedways'. Under this scheme each new development, like the Barbican Estate, effectively issued neighbouring property owners an ultimatum, to relocate their front door to the level of overpass bridges or in the future find that users of their buildings would be stepping into a basement, formerly known as the street. In other words: be a part of our utopian vision, *or else.*

There is a risk that the true lesson from stories like these can become overstated. The failure of London's Pedway Scheme does not

32
This concept, that humans consume the resources their descendants will need to survive, is articulated in the most memorable way by Tim Flannery. See: Tim Flannery, *The Future Eaters: An Ecological History of the Australasian Lands and People* (Sydney: New Holland Publishers, 2005).

33
Peter Blake, *Form Follows Fiasco: Why Modern Architecture Hasn't Worked* (Boston: Little Brown and Co., 1974).

34
Brent C. Brolin, *The Failure of Modern Architecture* (London: Studio Vista, 1976).

35
Tom Wolfe, *From Bauhaus to Our House* (London: Picador, 1981).

36
Charles Jencks, *The Language of Post-Modern Architecture*, (London: Academy Editions, [1977] 1987), 9-10.

37
I first discussed this
strategy for circumvent-
ing infinite regressions
in architectural theories
in my PhD dissertation,
then this following
paper: Steven Fleming,
'Theorising daylight:
Kahn's Unitarian Church
and Plato's super-Form,
The Good', Architectural
Research Quarterly, Vol. 10
(2006) No. 1, 25-36.

mean a permanent abnegation of citywide architectural thinking. The real message is that any one citywide vision, even if it catches on with most leaders, still needs to be able to coexist with, and show good manners toward, the citywide visions of others. The measure of a great utopian vision is not whether it rises to the top of the government's list of priorities, like pedways or carriageways, but whether or not that vision can coexist with those of our neighbours.

Let's see if that can be said of a cycling utopia. The first step will be to define that utopia in its pure-crystalline form, in the literary style of the utopian genre. The aim is to do for bike planning what More did for socialism with his novel *Utopia*, what Howard did for T.O.D. with his concept of Garden Cities, or what Wright did for sprawl with Broadacre, that is, provide a crystalline vision of a bicycle utopia. It seems perfectly reasonable in a world where a suburbanite's aim to spread out is appreciated by politicians and where a transit user's wish to live near a station is understood by the planning community, both with the help of pure models, that the goal of keen cyclists to have most of their transport requirements met by a bike should have a planning model to help them achieve that.

Note that the written description to follow will not be accompanied by a map of Velotopia, as it might look in the crystalline realm of our imagining, or in the real world should ever a dictator decide to build it in its entirety. There is a philosophical reason for this.

Think of the text in a cake recipe book. No one would point to one of the recipes, as written, and say 'that is a cake'. Pictures are different. Anyone pointing to a photo in a cake-recipe book is more likely to say 'that is a cake' than 'that is a photo of a cake'. It takes an odd mind, like René Magritte's, to do otherwise.

So what about a line of croquembouches at a cake judging competition? They all have something in common, the idea of the croquembouche. What is that idea? It would be tempting to produce a photo or a drawing of a croquembouche stripped to essentials, and call this the idea. Unfortunately, this introduces a problem of infinite regression. That's because now we can point to any of the croquembouches on the table and say 'that is a croquembouche', yet at the same time point to the drawing or photo and say 'that is croquembouche'. The croquembouches on the table and the drawing participate in a common idea. Do we draw an even simpler sketch of a croquembouche and call that the common idea? We could, but the new image can be called a croquembouche too, and so on, *ad infinitum*.

It would have been better if we had never produced a photo or drawing to start with, but referred to a written recipe as the idea. So long as the recipe didn't include any embellishments, we would broadly agree that all the croquembouches got to be on this judging table, and not on the table of sponge cakes, because they conformed to something we would all call a *recipe*, not a croquembouche.

This problem, that Aristotle identified in the thinking of Plato, rears its head in urban design theory whenever drawings are used to describe ideal-city plans.[37] If it only bothered philosophers, the problem could be ignored, but it is designers themselves who get caught in this

In English Magritte's caption reads 'This is not a pipe.'

Croquembouche

trap. Nothing they can actually build will look as elegant or complete as the picture they used to describe it. Like any of us trying to make a croquembouche while looking at a photo of one from a Pierre Hermé patisserie in Paris, they become dissatisfied with their own efforts, and are easy targets for critics.

# From a City for Driving to a City for Cycling

# proposition 3

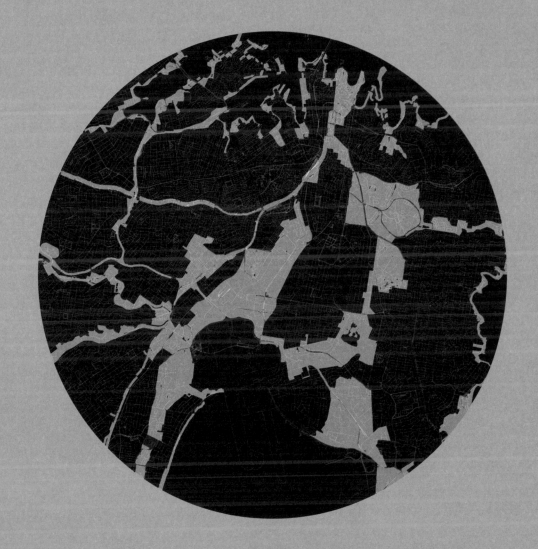

# Sydney

Most people living in Sydney see
gridlock and crowded trains, but
from a bicycle oriented development
standpoint it is possible to see
reserves and flat redevelopment sites
connected by non-vehicular easements
that can be made into greenways.

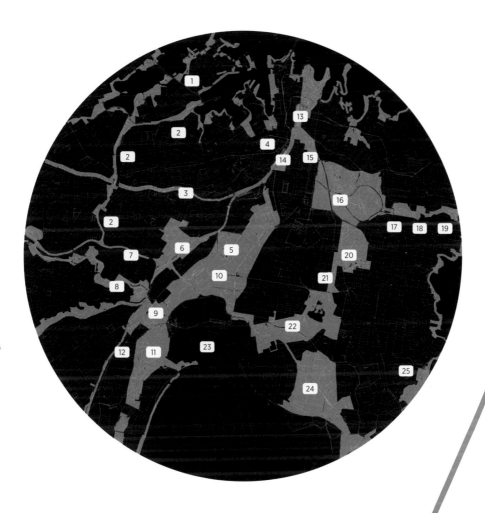

A 15km diameter circle captures potential redevelopment sites and easements for the bicycle highways needed to connect them all up. Riding at 15 kph, any slow cyclist could reach two thirds of the blue on this map within half an hour, provided their bike routes followed waterways and rail corridors so did not make them stop for car traffic.

1. Birchgrove foreshore - various parks
2. Inner-west light rail line
3. Inner-west main rail line
4. Tumbalong park/Darling Harbour
5. Sydney Park
6. Marrickville/St Peters Industrial Area
7. Bankstown Line
8. Cooks River - existing cycle path
9. Gough Whitlam Park / Cooks River
10. Alexandra Canal Industrial Area
11. Varoius connected parks stretching from Cooks river mouth to Rockdale

12. Carlingford Line
13. Hyde Park / Botanic Gardens
14. Central Station
15. Section of Surry Hills currently residential that would be needed to link the Western Velotopia with the East
16. Centennial Park
17. Queens Park
18. Queens Park to Bronte Link. As with Surry Hills, some current residential would need to be used to link to the beach.

19. Bronte Beach
20. Randwick Racecourse
21. Randwick to Botany link. As with Bronte and Surry Hills, small section of residential used.
22. Eastlakes Golf Course
23. Sydney Airport
24. Banksmeadow/Port Botany Industrial Area
25. Maroubra Beach

The proposal is for a bike-friendly apartment building at the epicentre of this circle, and a new 5km bike highway to Sydney's central train station, starting along Alexandria Canal.

Given Alexandria's importance to the city's logistics, a cyclelogistics distribution centre is proposed for the base of the building. Increasingly couriers in Europe are using pedelec trikes to bypass the restrictions and jams impeding the use of delivery vans.

A location 20 minutes by bike from a CBD
and near to a seaport and airport, is ideal
for a cyclelogistics warehouse and depot.
The other innovation, shown in this slide, is that
floor plates are organised around scissored
bike ramps serving every apartment.

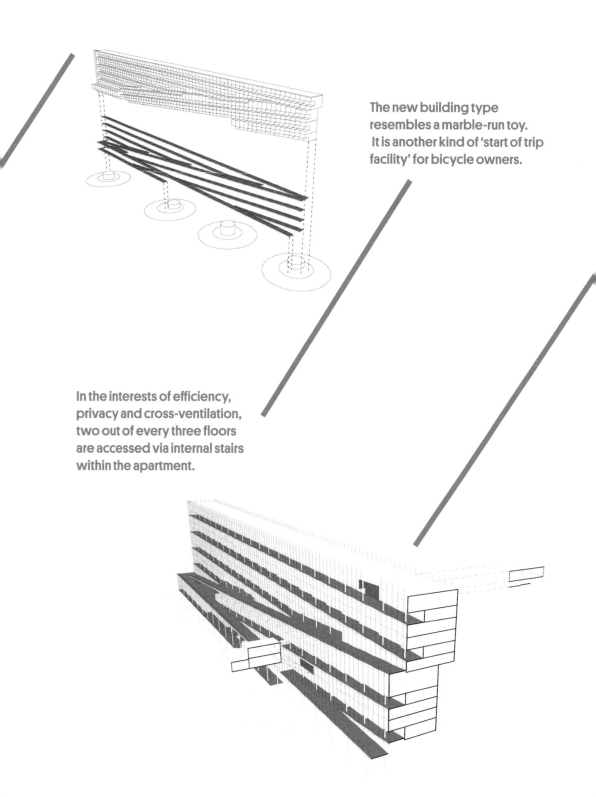

The new building type
resembles a marble-run toy.
It is another kind of 'start of trip
facility' for bicycle owners.

In the interests of efficiency,
privacy and cross-ventilation,
two out of every three floors
are accessed via internal stairs
within the apartment.

Only the half-sized entry levels open onto the ramped access galleries, that serve every third floor.

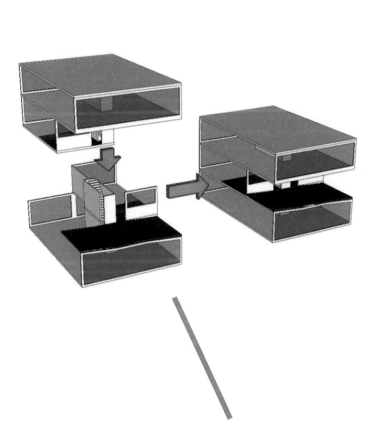

In saying NO to car parking, single-storey/single-aspect apartments, train travel and too many lifts, the project says YES to affordable housing, health and the environment, as well as speedy commutes and deliveries in the bikeable flat regions of Sydney.

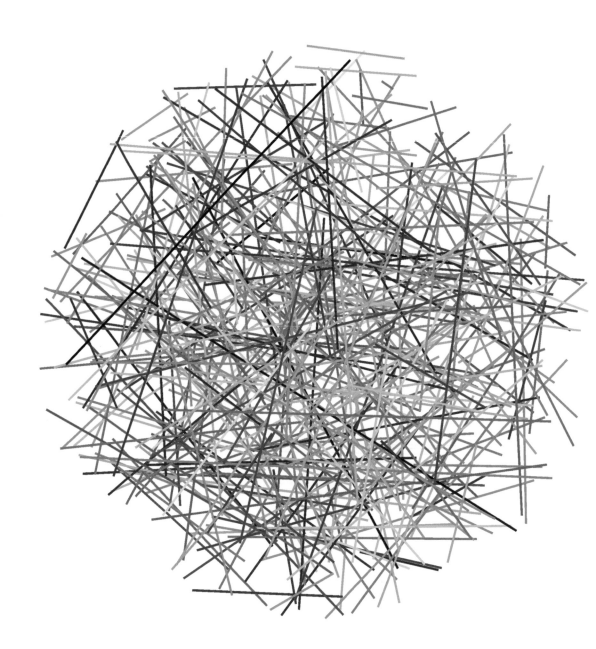

# chapter 3
# Velotopia

Velotopia is as circular as the topography has allowed,[1] for the usual reason that citizens are always clamouring to live near the civic centre. Development has been restricted to level ground, leaving any hills underdeveloped. Development has also been restricted to 15-km-diameter city limits. That ensures average commuting distances of less than 7 km and average trip times of less than 30 minutes by bike.

The 15-km limits define an area of 177 square kilometres. Development control guidelines are designed to ensure that at least 30,000 people live in every square kilometre, the average density across Manhattan (including the parks). One day as many as 6 million people will live here, with shorter average trip times, just using bikes, than they would have in any other city with that population.

1
Almost every ideal city model since Plato first imagined his ideal Polis in Laws has been circular by default. See: Plato, 'Laws', in: *The Dialogues of Plato*, translated by B. Jowett, Vol. 4 (Oxford: Clarendon Press, 1953). Unlike particular cities on earth that Plato might say are instances of many Ideas ('The Coast-line', for instance, making it crescent shaped like Chicago, or the Idea of 'The Mountain Range', making it sausage shaped like Barcelon – ideal cities exist in a realm beyond sensory apprehension and are not blended with any ideas that are not essential to the existence of every city.

2
J.H. Crawford,
*Carfree Cities* (Dublin:
International Books, 2000).

3
Keith Barry, 'New Helsinki
Bus Line Lets You Choose
Your Own Route', *Wired*,
(10 November 2013).
Available online: http://
www.wired.com/2013/10/
on-demand-public-transit/,
accessed 1 November 2014.

No disciples of Le Corbusier, Harvey Corbett, Robert Moses or Norman Bel Geddes have been to Velotopia. That means there are no highways and no racks of car-parking stations. Neither have any disciples of Ebenezer Howard been there to suggest that development be clustered around satellite towns with train connections back to the core. It is car-free yet ignores almost all of J.H. Crawford's ideas about Carfree Cities – a hard line interpretation of transit oriented development principles.[2]

Velotopia has never sought the services of mobility experts, so has no P&R (park and ride), ERP (electronic road pricing), PRT (personal rapid transport), HOV lanes (high-occupancy vehicle), LRT systems (light rail transit), or anything else that might seem essential because it is described by an acronym. All Velotopia has is a ground plane where nothing is allowed to threaten or obstruct cycling.

Whenever stakeholder groups are formed for consultation on matters of planning or public life, their constitution requires that the majority be primary-care givers of young children. There is no charity or positive discrimination at play here. They don't want to put the last first and the first last. They simply want to optimize conditions for a group that makes many trips in a day and whose work (raising the next generation) has a great influence on the city's wealth and productivity in the long term.

Successive committees of parents have voted against a rail network throughout the city, worrying the speed of those trains, as well as their length and their actual tracks, might bother them when they are riding their box bikes or riding with children cycling beside them. It is sufficient, they have said, to have a few electric carts, the kind that move the disabled through airports, available to collect them at times when they are physically unable to cycle. Advances in technology mean these are now driverless carts, powered by batteries, charged from the sun.

It has been important to them as well that those carts not be fitted with roofs. Any measures to keep public transport users dry should keep cyclists dry too. Attaching roofs to vehicles would only absolve Velotopia's leaders of their responsibility to ultimately roof-over key routes through the city to give cyclists an opportunity to seek protection from the sun and the rain. Here's how it is written in their constitution: 'Comfort and convenience is a public resource, evenly distributed through all architecture. Carriages (cars, trams, etcetera) have nothing extra to offer.'

It is for this reason that Velotopia has a small but efficient fleet of electric carts running like carts in an airport, or Helsinki's mini-bus service.[3] They are not as convenient as riding a bike because of the requirement to call one then wait for it to arrive. They are also expensive for those not carrying disability cards, so tend not to be used if a bike or

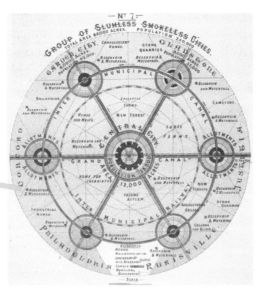

Ebeneza Howard's Garden City

Crawford's Six-Lobe City

Electric cart

Roundabout

Disney behind the scenes

a cargo bike could be an option. Neither are they fast, being limited to 15 kph. That is to ensure that they always fall in behind bicycle traffic. Nevertheless, they benefit from the city's smooth flowing traffic. It may be slow, but it never has to slow down or stop, so in the end connectivity speed is much faster. The city doesn't need any traffic lights as there is no risk of any high-speed collisions. What they have are small round-abouts, typically raised on elevated mounds. Rising onto the mounds bikes naturally shed enough speed to safety filter through, before naturally regaining their lost speed as they descend on their way.

But it is not the absence of traffic lights that really strikes visitors of Velotopia. What astounds them is the almost complete absence of powered transport machines, in a city on its way to having 6 million people!

There is a major subway station in the centre of the city, covered with ground level shops. Above those is a giant structure for parking thousands of bikes. But trains departing this station don't leave to other parts of the city. There is no local network. No metro map can be seen on its walls. All of the trains that depart from Velotopia Station are bound for other cities.

Dotted around Velotopia, outside city limits, are car-parking garages. Visitors coming from car-centric parts of the region park their cars here and swap to one of the four legal modes – cycling, walking, pedicabs or the dynamically routed driverless carts – to enter the city. Although most Velotopians heading out of the city go on their bikes, some hire cars from these points on the outskirts if they need to go to the country.

With regards to essential services, non-urgent patient transport is done with modified pedicabs and police do patrols using bikes. Deliveries to houses and small shops are all managed using the same cycle-logistics methods that have been developed in European towns to side-step laws that ban vans after 10 A.M.. Tradespeople, cleaning contractors, gardeners and other groups who can't prove they need to carry more than 500 kg for their work, are likewise compelled to use cargo bikes.

As a result, and even though it is a city of millions, there are never more than a few dozen heavy vehicles moving throughout Velotopia at any one time – not enough to warrant a network of service roads. Successive committees of stakeholders (parents) have been very particular about not wanting service roads. People here don't want to be superficially car-free, while cars serve their needs in some behind-the-scenes way. They say that would be like living on Main Street, U.S.A. in Disneyland where visitors are let to believe there are no vehicles, rubbish collections or hurried staff, and that all of the shops are somehow stocked using magic. Disneyland's deceit is only possible thanks to an underground network of utility corridors.

Given the opportunity to hide vehicular movements underground or on service roads hidden behind buildings, the temptation would have always existed to allow a few vans, then a few motorized taxis, and before anyone knew it the city could have been dependent on more vehicular movements than anybody could count. They have always preferred for their ration of machines to remain in the light, where each can be scrutinized.

The people of Velotopia know that garbage trucks collect their bulk waste. They see the cranes and cement mixers that build their new buildings. They are aware that trucks service their supermarkets. It is precisely because motorized vehicles are put in plain view, where they sometimes annoy them, that the people of Velotopia would never vote for a mayor who allowed the ration of motorized vehicles to ever increase.

That leaves fire trucks, ambulances and police cars. These all have 15-kph speed-limiting devices just as the trucks do, but they can move at full speed under siren. Emergency vehicles make better time than they would in a city of cars thanks to Velotopia's compactness and the ease with which cyclists are able to get out of their way.

That covers the broad-brush proscriptions and planning measures, arrived at by designers who listened to committees of parenting stake-holders and who employed collectivist thinking.

As to its urban design (meaning permissible building envelopes, onuses on developers, public-realm principles, etcetera), Velotopia is unlike any kind of city hitherto seen, which surprises most people. Ever since Jane Jacobs started a rebellion against the radical urban forms that evolved in response to the car, most had assumed that designing cities for people, instead of machines, would mean a simple return to the urban mor-phologies and public spaces of the pre-automobile city. But Velotopia is something else again. It is a bicycling city. The best way to explain its uniqueness is by pointing out particular oddities that set it apart from a nineteenth-century city. Manhattan from 14th Street to 125th Street provides the best known point of reference by which to explain.

The so-called De Witt plan, or Commissioner's Plan of 1811, has frequent streets across the short width of Manhattan and infrequent avenues running its length. It seems absurd that someone standing mid-block on a street cannot move north or south until they have walked 100 m to the east or the west to the nearest avenue. That is until you realize an advantage of spacing avenues so far apart: that merchants know where to set up their shops to catch passing trade. Shops line the avenues. They don't line the streets. And although pedestrians might occasionally complain about the length of the blocks, at least they know where to find all the stores.

This focus on funnelling pedestrians along a scarcity of avenues is

Protected bike lane, 8th Avenue, New York. Photo: David Holowka

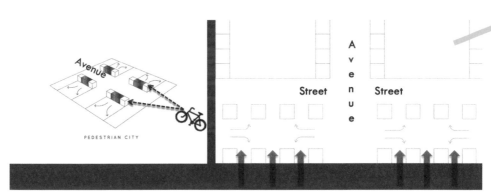

Diffusion of shops

what will stop Manhattan ever being an ideal stage for bicycle mobility. Consider it from the merchants' perspective. If Manhattan became a city where everyone left home with a bike, the merchants with mid-block locations on the avenues would lose their exposure. Where right now their patrons pass by at 3-5 kph and are able to see each narrow shop front, bicycling patrons passing at between 15 and 25 kph only see shops as a blur. The only merchants capturing the eye of bike-riding shoppers are the ones with corner locations.

In Velotopia every commercial premises has a corner location. It is as if one day all the disgruntled shopkeepers lining the avenues had picked up their shops, relocated them part-way along their nearest side streets, then finished their day by quadrupling the number of avenues.

While street life in Velotopia isn't concentrated but diffused, overall numbers of passers-by are even higher for shopkeepers here than on avenues in Manhattan. That's because moving in this city is fun. People make more discretionary trips. Half of the time they're moving through the city for no reason other than to be out. For merchants it's like having a kiosk in the middle of an ice rink with prospective patrons randomly swirling around them. Every patron has between 10 and 15 seconds to notice their shop, travelling at between 4 and 5 m per second.

From the point of view of citizens riding their bikes, it is a great relief not being herded to avenues and funnelled along them. The shops are like giant pilotis holding apartment buildings and office buildings aloft in the air, so the ground plane feels like a continuous meadow.

Earlier attempts to build 'towers in a park' (as Le Corbusier had branded the concept) were sabotaged by ready-slum-making policies and acres of asphalt for the storage of cars – so much for the park! But in Velotopia the ground plane is productive. Apart from the fine rhizome trace-work of cycle tracks that cover the city, every other centimetre of space has been given either to habitats for local wildlife, urban farming or play areas to benefit the citizens' physical and mental wellbeing.

The predominance of perimeter blocks held in the air by piloti-like shops would make it a difficult city to find your way around, but the ground plane of Velotopia is infinitely varied. Cities with cars may be diverse in their architectural forms and the widths of their streets. Look down, though, and all you will see is the same tired asphalt, curbs and lane markings. In Velotopia there are smooth tracks that attract skaters, dirt tracks with berms and jumps designed for mountain bike riders and more paving treatments than you could fit in a catalogue.

At first it is hard to image how garbage trucks or cement mixers ever move through the city. Then you notice the pairs of parallel paths set as far apart as their wheels.

As mentioned, development eschews hills and is concentrated on level ground. That flat plane, though, has been contoured. The shops all sit on top of earth mounds so that cyclists naturally slow down as they approach them, and naturally speed up as they ride away. There is a saying here that high means slow, and low means go.[4] High points are where bikes slow to a speed suitable for mingling with pedestrians, while the low spaces between are for bikes to move at cruising speed.

So how do pedestrians move between shops? In parts of Velotopia that have turned out to be busier because of a conglomeration of popular attractions, the preference is for grade separation. Light weight bridges link the crests of the mounds so that pedestrians can walk over while cyclists ride underneath. The few bridges that require them have lifting mechanisms to allow heavy vehicles to pass under. Throughout most of Velotopia, though, cyclists and pedestrians convivially share the same space.

People looking at Velotopia from places where cars are still viewed as freedom machines say Velotopia's laws represent a deprivation of liberty. It appals them to see people not being free to drive cars in their own city. But as far as the people of Velotopia are concerned, critics of their laws have been hoodwinked by car and oil companies. As Velotopians see it, car and oil companies are like gun manufacturers. The gun industry would love it if their products were embraced as symbols of liberty. They would love it if target shooting on city streets we as normal as pedestrians having cars hurtle past them with nothing but a raised curb for protection. Granting gun owners that liberty would impinge on other peoples' liberty to feel safe on the street. Velotopians extend that logic to owners of cars.

To summarize, here is the ingredients list for the Velotopia recipe:
- High-density housing over a permeable ground plane
- Sited on relatively flat land with any hills left undeveloped
- 15 km diameter city limits
- A gravity-forced transit plane where cyclists can cross the city as the crow flies
- Pedestrian networks and shared space on the crests of mounds linked by pedestrian bridges
- Roundabouts raised on slight mounds
- Buildings organized around spiralling ramps
- Freed of all encumbrances to bike movement, like cars
- Largely protected from the sun and the rain

4
'High means slow' and 'low means go' are slogans coined by four students who undertook one of my bicycle-focused design studios: Sara Chugg, Rachel Englund, Fiona McMullen and Chivonne Prouse.

# From Brownfields to Bike Fields

# proposition 4

# Newcastle

Newcastle has enough post-industrial wastelands to accommodate an equal population of apartment dwellers who cycle, and enough non-vehicular public space for them to ride between redevelopment districts in safety.

Redeveloping wastelands with high density housing on a bicycle mobility platform could relieve population pressure on neighbouring Sydney, without recreating Sydney's congestion.

## Space of no consequence to driving

## Proposed Green Loop

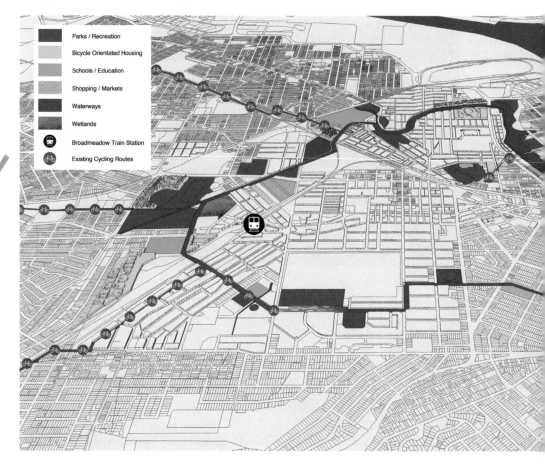

Parks / Recreation

Bicycle Orientated Housing

Schools / Education

Shopping / Markets

Waterways

Wetlands

Broadmeadow Train Station

Existing Cycling Routes

Let's start the process with a saleable idea, one that dyed-in-the-wool suburbanites can embrace without loving cycling or high density living.

The proposal starts with a green loop connecting redevelopment sites. It would follow naturalised waterways and connect the loose ends of the city's four main cycleways. It is envisaged that progressives moving to new developments (here coloured yellow) would not own their own cars, but use share cars for trips to less bike-friendly parts of the city.

This slide zooms in on Bicycle Oriented Development (B.O.D.) opportunities in Wickham and Maryville. Proposed cycling corridors follow waterways and the routes of former industrial rail lines where easements remain.

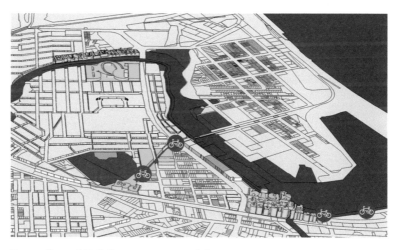

Details of BOD opportunities

In addition to more practical bike parking solutions: Broadmeadow station is the natural departure point for train trips to Sydney. Besides more practical bike parking solutions an Automated Storage/Retrieval System (AS/RS), clad in glass, would help to celebrate cycling.

High capacity bike parking is also useful in areas that draw crowds, such as beaches in Summer, and sites of temporary markets, like this site at the beginning of Hunter Street Mall.

Such structures in each of the pictured locations along the main street would serve as beacons to drivers, inviting them to cycle instead, and serve the peak parking needs of this linear strip of crowd-drawing venues and sites.

Mark MacLean, author of *A Year Down the Drain*, speaks to community members surveying the Newcastle Waterway Discovery Loop.

However, the centrepiece of the proposal remains the 'waterway discovery loop'. From its grassroots origins it has has drawn together community leaders to tour the loop and speak to issues of memory, ecology and bicycle advocacy.

Serving public
gathering places with
bike parking stations

**chapter 4**

# Real World
# Issues

Christiania

## Velo-heterotopia

Now that we have defined a utopian model we need to see if its rules can be played on the field of an actual city without quashing other peoples' visions that may be informed by Broadacre, Garden Cities and Futurama. The thinking is that the Velotopia model just needs a foothold in cities to start with. It only needs to exist on one layer. When it does, though, it will provide an alternative model. The hope is that it would draw people to relocate for a better life. It could influence the redevelopment of formerly car-centric districts. It could be the inspiration for cities built entirely from scratch.

What it can't be is a model that has to be imposed upon people who don't catch the vision. That was the problem with London's Pedway Scheme. It was totalizing. Either it would succeed in bringing every other building's entry to the level of a new network of pedways, or it would be worthless. There couldn't be any half measures.

Is the Velotopia model one that can coexist with models based on machine transportation, but without being diluted? We will see that it can, but it needs its own clearly defined space in the city.

Attentive students of architectural theory and urban geography will be familiar with Michel Foucault's ruminations about heterotopias.[1] They are certainly helpful here. Literally translated, heterotopia means 'other place' – the word 'other' being typically loaded. Think of spaces like monasteries, prisons, theme parks and asylums with internal orders that deviate radically from the dominant order of the world outside their boundaries or walls.

Foucault's idea that heterotopic spaces are ones that stand in opposition to hegemonies reminds us that the idea of Velotopia, if it were superimposed on an actual city, could give rise to spaces (or moreover chains of spaces linked by greenways and trails) that needn't be integrated into car-dependent parts of the city. Rather we can imagine the car-focused city and the bike-focused city having their backs to each other. Movement between them would be via gateways or thresholds.

The car-free island of Sark in the Channel Islands as well as the Toronto Islands in Canada are decisively separated by bodies of water from the car-dominated regions on which they depend for employment and trade. In both cases a ferry serves as a gate. Similarly removed from its context is the bicycle and pedestrian district of Freetown Christiania in Copenhagen. The automotive order of Copenhagen is held at bay by old military defences and stone bollards placed with no regard for their impact on emergency vehicles.

At the other end of the spectrum are places that motorists are able to enter by car, but rarely do due to unfavourable traffic engineering approaches. The car-free neighbourhood of Vauban in Freiburg, Germany has no barriers physically preventing cars from coming inside. It simply allows drivers nowhere to stop. Likewise cars can enter the central district of Amsterdam, but are likely to be stuck behind courier trucks if they do. In the case of Velotopian districts emplaced within car-dominated cities, removable and/or hydraulic bollards would likely be a common sight around thresholds.

1
Michel Foucault, 'Different Spaces', in: Michel Foucault, *Aesthetics, Method and Epistemology*, translated by Robert Hurley (London: Allen Lane, [1967/1985] 1998), 298-300.

2
Colin Rowe and Fred
Koetter, *Collage City*
(Cambridge, MA: The MIT
Press,1979).

Foucault's observation that certain heterotopic spaces including amuse-
ment parks and prisons literally or metaphorically require tickets for
entry will assuage our unease about Velotopian spaces having an air of
exclusivity. Yes, there is a ticket to full citizenship: you need a bike. That's
not to say a blind person, or someone so poor that they don't own a bike,
or someone so disabled that no human-powered contraption can serve
them, will be ignored. Subsidized public transport options would be available to them. But let's be honest, just like in a car city, they would not be
the ones whose needs get top priority. So yes, the bike is a ticket.

Having to own a bike, though, is hardly as onerous as needing a car
to gain the best access to your city. And consider the benefits to pedestrians of living in a city where cyclists and pedestrians are separated the
way motorists are separated from vulnerable road users. It would be
cyclists who are separated from pedestrians, eliminating conflicts arising
from the two belonging to the same category (as they do currently), and
eliminating a raft of greater impositions upon pedestrians brought on
by the presence of cars in the city: noise, collisions occasioning death,
pollution, cars parked over footpaths, drivers bullying their way across
footpaths into garages, etcetera. Where the car is the ticket, the stakes
are much higher.

As tickets go, a cheap bike and a body made strong by regular riding are within reach of virtually everyone, even those in relative poverty.
One only need compare the broad cross-section of society enjoying inde-
pendent transport in the Netherlands with the narrow cross section of
people fully served by car-centric design. Without a job, perfect eyesight
and skills to pass driving tests, you're on the outer.

Another of Foucault's ideas, that a heterotopic space is in some
sense always a psychological construct, reminds us that any manifestation of Velotopia in the real world would be more recognizable to a
person in the habit of going by bike than someone who is in the habit of
walking, driving or taking the bus or the train. One can imagine non-cyclists walking into spaces that are crucial to the pursuit of the bicycling
lifestyle without even knowing. We see this already. Tourists on Brooklyn
Bridge in New York amble all over the marked cycle track with no idea
they are blocking a crucial transport corridor for thousands of cyclists.

A picture is emerging of a kind of space that is more like oil in a lava
lamp than a dye that changes the colour of a whole city. Town planners
don't like separatist thinking. They prefer messiness and blending – the
Jane Jacobs prescription. The problem is that having cars in the mix is
like having black watercolour paint on your brush. The slightest trace
turns everything the colour of ash.

Architects' contributions to urban design theory aren't so strictly opposed
to separatist thinking, and often work with it. Take Colin Rowe's book
*Collage City*.[2] Like steel-truss calculations and crits in front of the class,
that book was like a bed of hot coals that a whole generation of architects
were made to walk over. If they survived the pompous Ruskinian prose
and gratuitous referencing, they would come away with two pearls of
wisdom: first that it's okay to have an each-way bet by designing different
parts of the city in different ways; and second that architectural projects

can be 'theatres of prophesy'.[3] According to Rowe there are theatres of prophesy and theatres of memory. The former are utopian emplacements that help the public imagine a new kind of future. The latter are things like gothic cathedrals that help people imagine the past.

3 Ibid., 49.

We would be setting ourselves up for disappointment if we hoped to redeem every part of every car city for parents with children and box bikes. It is more realistic aiming to build demonstration projects, 'theatres of prophesy', that give the public a taste for purpose built cycling environments.

Four demonstration projects have been proposed: for New York, Copenhagen, Sydney and the regional city of Newcastle, Australia. They each rub the wrong way with some long-standing attitudes, both societally and among experts in the built-environment planning community that need to be probed for bias and logic. We will then ask where similar redevelopment space might be found in another four cities: one post-industrial (Detroit), one planned (Canberra), one that has left its lowlands underdeveloped (Brisbane) and one with a medieval town centre (Amsterdam).

## Proposition 1:
## Chelsea-Elliot Bike-Lovers Houses in New York

For a city assumed to be saturated with development and traffic, New York has a surprising number of linear routes that aren't being used to move cars, open green space that could support more bike tracks, and potential redevelopment sites. The map shows how a 15-km-wide circle can be positioned to capture the bulk of that space, as well as midtown and downtown.

Originally conceived as a place for walking, Manhattan north of 14th Street has a grid that funnels people down a limited number of avenues. This way shop keepers know where to place their shops to intercept passers-by, and people walking know where to go to find shops.

It is hypothesized with this proposition that redeveloping the Chelsea-Elliot Houses site along purely bike-centric lines would mean taking the shops that cyclists can't see on the avenues and using them to bring life to the side streets, quadrupling the number of routes for moving north-south and sculpting the ground plane so that cyclists ride in low channels and stop upon crests where entries to buildings should be located. The walls of the shops could be load-bearing and used to suspend apartment buildings off of the ground. Voila: a ground plane on which cyclists can move as the crow flies.

Pedestrians, people in wheelchairs and slower cyclists would be separated from faster cyclists via an elevated network of pedways connecting the crests. Above all this there would be spiralling apartment blocks and canopies protecting cyclists from the worst of the weather.

If the environment emerging from this logical sequence of thoughts seems unacceptably dissimilar to the pedestrian-centric streetscapes urban designers have been advocating since the time of Jane Jacobs and

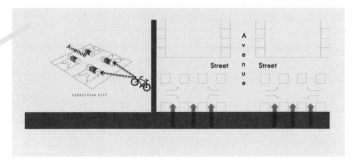

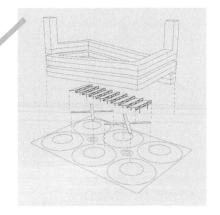

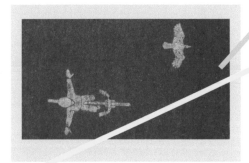

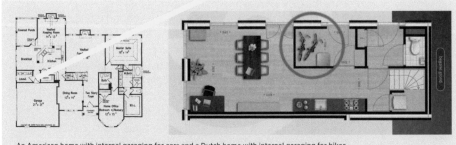

An American home with internal garaging for cars and a Dutch home with internal garaging for bikes.

Kevin Lynch, consider a remark by Robin Williams – the departed movie star, comedian and cycling enthusiast – that to him cycling was as close as we can get to feeling as though we can fly.[4] Anyone who can remember the moment when they first learned to cycle can probably relate. Now ask yourself this: if 6 million birds built a city, would their city have streets? If 6 million people all planning to ride bikes almost all of the time built a city, would they start with anything so regimenting, banal and 'pedestrian' as a nineteenth-century grid?

It bears mentioning too that the purpose of a book such as this is not to design actual projects. The aim is to imagine how built-environment planning might evolve if given as many decades to revolve around cycling as it has had since the 1950s to revolve around driving. No one could foretell in the 1950s exactly how that project would run.

The first thing to say about the design of the actual apartments is that designing with the bicycle in mind can make it just as fast and convenient leaving an upper level apartment as it always has been to leave a house on the ground. In the suburbs people have garages with automatic doors that open directly into their kitchens. Loading and unloading things like baby car seats or groceries is as streamlined as the building can make it. If suburbanites face any great inconvenience, it is the impossible length of most trips for walking and cycling, and the infrequency of public transport.

As densities go up certain conveniences fall away, but distances shorten. Presently a kind of sweet spot for cyclists can be found in medium-density districts and cities based on row housing. They are dense enough to put people within cycling reach of a few 100,000 people, or, if they ride to the nearest metro station, a few million more. London is a good example. You can get around your own borough by bike, or ride to the train station to access any point in the city. Best of all, as a cyclist, you have some of the convenience the motorist enjoys in the suburbs with their internal-access locked garage. You can wheel your bike through your front door to the kitchen. In the Netherlands some terrace houses at the ends of rows have a small internal-access locked garage just large enough for bikes.

The problem is that row housing cannot yield densities sufficient to stop a mega city sprawling beyond biking limits. But what if we take a terrace row, tilt it as though it were built on a 3-degree slope (that's still wheelchair accessible), then twist it into a spiral? It is possible to imagine the convenience of the terrace row being combined with the density of the multi storey perimeter block.

To minimize the ratio of circulation space to private living space, the spiralling access gallery can serve maisonette flats that cross over and under the gallery. A gallery that serves three levels like this can be three times as wide as a regular gallery without spoiling the efficiency of the plan. That's wide enough for riding, walking and perhaps some orderly bike parking.

Here you see a diagram of a 120-m-long single-helical perimeter block (40-m wide) as well as a diagram indicating how another helix can

4
'"The Closest You Can Get to Flying" – Cycling World Pays Tribute to Robin Williams', available online: http://revolights.com/blogs/news/15129449-the-closest-you-can-get-to-flying-cycling-world-pays-tribute-to-robin-williams, accessed 18 February 2015.

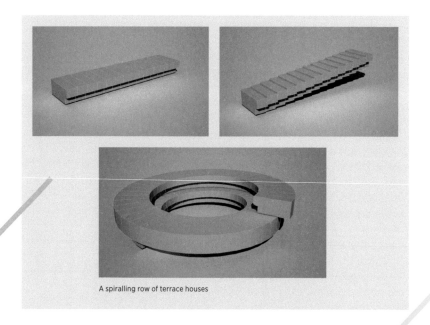

A spiralling row of terrace houses

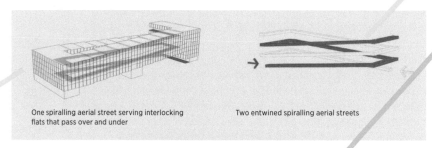

One spiralling aerial street serving interlocking
flats that pass over and under

Two entwined spiralling aerial streets

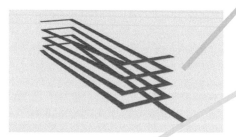

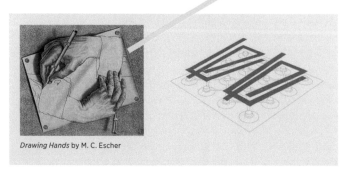

*Drawing Hands* by M. C. Escher

be intertwined if this block type is to be scaled-up to the length of a city block in Manhattan.

Without an intertwined helix a building with so great a circumference as a Manhattan block would have very shallow, 1.5-degree ramps and require four revolutions to ride to the bottom. Adding an intertwined helix means cyclists can go from the top to the bottom of 12-storey Manhattan 'blockbuster' with just two revolutions on 3-degree ramps.

Doubtless there would be discombobulation among some first-time visitors to a building with four lift stops, 12 storeys and two 'levels' that don't remain at the same height. Imagine descending. After one revolution of the courtyard you will have magically missed two levels of galleries that you could reasonably have assumed your path would include. It could be like a trip on a strange loop, a mathematical and psychological entity Douglas Hofstadter describes in his book *Gödel, Escher, Bach*,[5] but instead of feeling as though you were spiralling and arriving back at the point from which you began, you will have reached the ground with half the number of revolutions you had assumed would be needed.

Raising the apartment blocks on the structural walls of the shops means their monolithic size makes no difference to the new district's permeability, either for cyclists moving on the lowest level or pedestrians following the diagonal grid of bridges linking the crests.

The Chelsea-Elliot Houses site falls within a part of New York with a diameter of 15 km, chosen here for having an abundance of linear easements that aren't used by motoring voters, and space people would rarely head to by train or by car. That is space that can be redeveloped with the Velotopia model in mind. It doesn't need to be cleared of cars. It's largely car-free already. Queens especially has an abundance of rail easements tracing back to a time when competing industrialists were duplicating rail infrastructure. It is incredible that some of those easements, like the former Rockaway Beach Branch line, have not been made into greenways already.[6] Other possible routes include air space above active rail routes, paths crossing cemeteries and encased creeks that could be naturalized ('daylit').

Accounting for circuity, the average commuting distance in the blue space might be 10 km – more than the 7 km that could be achieved if the whole city were redeveloped in the manner proposed for the Chelsea-Elliot Houses site. The average commute time for the slower (15-kph) cyclists could therefore be as short as 40 minutes, less than the average in London.

Can't a lot of the black space be navigated already by bike? Of course it can, but not with as much ease as the blue space if it were redeveloped within a bike-transport framework. New York's cycle tracks blend bike and car traffic at intersections and make cyclists moving targets for motorists entering driveways. Cyclists are also slowed down by traffic lights that would not need to be there if it weren't for car traffic. Cycling is possible but within a machine-city framework. The aim here is to imaging heterotopias, or 'theatres of prophecy' as Rowe would say, that are inspiring enough to be beacons of change.

You will note too that this grand scheme does not radiate out from either of the New York's established centres of business. Each of

5
Douglas Hofstadter, *Gödel, Escher, Bach: An Eternal Golden Braid* (New York: Basic Books, 1979).

6
A report recommending this line be converted into a greenway would now be forgotten were it not for a volunteer lobby group. See: http://thequeensway.org/.

7
Kenneth T. Jackson,
*Crabgrass Frontier: The
Suburbanization of the
United States* (Oxford:
Oxford University Press,
1987).

these are where they are due to the logic of transport modes other than cycling. Downtown grew from where boats used to dock in the seventeenth century. The office blocks of midtown Manhattan clamber around Grand Central Station. It therefore makes sense that people pursuing the Velotopia dream in New York find their own centre according to the logic of cycling. In this case it might be in the vicinity of Newtown Creek, including the industrial land on either side, and the first and new Calvary cemeteries in Queens.

Cyclists riding in from the periphery of a 15-km-across zone would not be looking for the same kind of centre that pedestrians look for as they step from a train. Geometrically, the bicyclists' centre is a focal zone generated by people looking inward from a circumference. Midtown Manhattan is the opposite. It grew in annular waves out from a nucleus, the doors exiting Grand Central Station. As to the size of both kinds of centres, the imperative for compactness in a walking-based business district like midtown Manhattan squeezes out housing. Towers fill with office space only. But imagine midtown without Grand Central Station and everyone arriving from surrounding districts by bike, a mode that increases their speed by five times. Theoretically, a centre for cyclists could be five-times greater in diameter and 25-times greater in area. The offices we see stacked in 25-storey towers in midtown could all be spread out on the ground. That would leave the upper levels of all the buildings available for apartments.

The scenario described is one that can be observed in the centre of Amsterdam, where there is no business district per se. There may be some clusters of entertainment venues and shops, but office space is interspersed amidst housing. Even in Zuidas, which has been purpose-built as a business district with its own metro station, the shrinking effect bikes have on space means offices are spread across a large area and space in between is attracting residential development.

Because cycling is one-fifth the speed of driving, and five times the speed of walking, we should expect the centres of bike-centric cities will be halfway between the totally decentralized city that Kenneth Jackson says we end up with when planning revolves around driving[7] and the model that is produced by train stations and slowness of walking, exemplified by midtown.

We've seen three impressions of the ground plane, showing people and vegetation to give the space between buildings the feeling of being lived-in. Since a far smaller portion of the space between buildings will be needed to deal with traffic than is needed when traffic means cars, we can imagine most of that space being put to productive and recreational uses like urban farms, restored habitats for original wildlife, aquaculture, playgrounds, etcetera.

Magazines and websites of interest to urbanists have become saturated with artists' impressions with these kinds of features, largely masking conventional, machine-dependent building types in the background. But pretty pictures are not the way to foreground salient new building types and urban morphological patterns. Neither does it seem to be the way to change the course of city growth. The last urban design visions

Castello Plan, New Amsterdam

From Proposition 1, page 26

Vertical City, Ludwig Hilberseimer, 1927

Plan Voisin, Le Corbusier

From Proposition 1, page 31

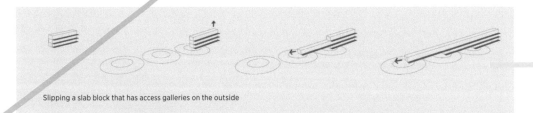

Slipping a slab block that has access galleries on the outside

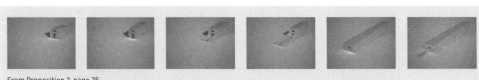

From Proposition 2, page 76

that reversed the way we all think about cities, in the way we need to reverse our thinking again if we are to meet the challenge of global warming, were stark and uncompromising. Like Ludwig Hilberseimer's Vertical City of 1924, they left out vegetation to draw attention to the thing that was new, in that case cars at ground level and pedestrians on podium roofs and flyover bridges.

More influential still was Le Corbusier's Plan Voisin of 1925. Some renders showed greenery, but with his most memorable and influential images Le Corbusier employed the technique of contradistinction to shock us into absorbing ideas that were totally new. The proliferation of his vision in so many countries tell us his strategy worked. Perhaps shock can work now too.

Following Le Corbusier's game plan means presenting the redevelopment proposal for the Chelsea-Elliot Houses in a way that starkly contrasts its familiar surroundings. Architects understand that mega blocks can be designed with decoration and/or articulation and not look quite so monolithic, but the public may not. For their benefit, and for the purposes of accelerating a paradigm shift, it may be better to present the proposal in a way that Le Corbusier showed can garner attention.

## Proposition 2:
## Unite d' Bicycle Nation in Copenhagen

The proposition for Copenhagen is less about that city than possible modifications to a building type that is generally reviled for its associations with the meanest public housing estates that were built in the wake of the Second World War, namely, the very long slab block. It is a building type, though, that is likely to go on being built due to some undeniable benefits: principally, the way it allows us to build for the disabled with no walk-up apartment blocks, without making those apartments unduly expensive. That is because the cost of a lift can be shared by many apartments.

Our focus with this proposition is the way the slab block can be tilted then have its floors 'slipped' to meet the ground. A new building type is created, referred to here as a 'slip block'. Here you see a sequence showing how the slipping operation might look when performed on a single-loaded slab block with access galleries on the outside.

More efficient still are double-loaded slab blocks like the ones proposed here for Copenhagen. Not only do their lifts have many residents to chip in for their upkeep, but their corridors have twice as many sponsors as well: one apartment on either side.

It is not necessarily the case either that such a block will have a sunny side and dark side. If we orientate the long sides to the east and the west, every apartment can be given some sun, either in the morning or the afternoon, even on the shortest of days. Poor cross-ventilation, the weakness with this type, isn't so important in an extreme northern location like Copenhagen as the year-long guarantee of sunlight to every apartment.

8
E.L. Doctorow, *World's Fair: A Novel* (Random House, 2007).

9
Betty Friedan, *The Feminine Mystique* (New York: W.W. Norton, 2013).

10
See: Leslie Kanes Weisman, 'Women's Environmental Rights: A Manifesto', in: Jane Rendell, Barbara Penner and Iain Borden (Eds.), *Gender Space Architecture: An Interdisciplinary Introduction* (London: Routledge, 2000), 1-5.

When we discuss the next proposition, for Sydney, we will see how slip blocks don't need to be as long as the ones we are seeing, and can be stacked. We are looking at the simplest variant to begin with in order to focus on the question of why. Why tilt blocks so their corridors run to the ground? What is wrong with walking to a lift and leaving bikes parked on the ground? The reason, and the ultimate goal of the slip block, is to make our hypothetical mother's life easier than the life she might be tempted by in the suburbs. Since the car and sprawl project began it has been targeting mothers with claims of convenience that we need to combat.

## Happy Wife, Happy Life

The 1939 'Futurama' exhibition obviously had some masterful tricks of persuasion to make much of the world's population suddenly believe they could shift from walking, train travel and riding their bikes to a car-based model of urbanism. So what were its tricks, and can those tricks of persuasion be redeployed to inspire the next radical shift in our culture? One trick that stands out was how the Futurama pushed all the right buttons with mothers.

A passage in E.L. Doctorow's memoir *World's Fair* shows the young protagonist's father coming away from the 'Futurama' exhibition feeling sceptical about taxpayers' money being spent to build roads for General Motors.[8] It was his mother who Doctorow recalls whispering – so her husband would not overhear – that seeing the exhibition had made her now wish they owned a car.

General Motors sold the car-focused city the same way they sold their cars. They addressed husbands, fully aware that wives vet and/or make major household decisions. With one roof and five seats, the car would serve her goal of keeping the family together.

The irony is women have never been unhappier than after their move to the suburbs. Betty Friedan interviewed American housewives in the 1950s and decided the whole idea of women possessing a 'feminine mystique' enabling them to feel contented at home, stranded, while their husbands drove to work and their children took buses to school, was a media myth, created by men.[9] Women were miserable trapped in the suburbs.

Friedan's work was a catalyst for the second great wave of feminism, but what did that deliver for women? It didn't change the model of urban development, as feminist architectural critics have been keen to point out.[10] If we think purely in terms of mobility – a prime cause of housewives' unhappiness in the late 1950s – we can say Women's Liberation won equal rights for women to drive, the right to jobs to earn money for fuel and all the other costs of car ownership and the honour of driving their kids to football and netball.

While the same generation of women in the Netherlands and Denmark were protesting during the 1970s for separate bike infrastructure so their kids could make their own way to practice, mothers in the U.S., Australia, the U.K. and elsewhere were soaking in car manufacturers' ads. What a terrible duping!

A whole chapter could go here on the evils of cars and just how much we pay for our reliance upon them. Others, though, have covered that

Futurama expo

Levittown

Stop the child murder

Subaru Advert Soccer Mom

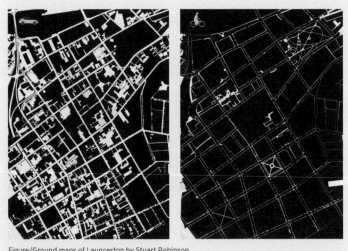

Figure/Ground maps of Launceston by Stuart Robinson,
Chau Hin Lim Charles, James Ho and Hakim Ahmat.

Apartment layout                              Bike accessible shop

Undulating paved landscapes

subject, brilliantly, but always with a tone of despair.[11] Now that cities have been built around cars, people naturally prefer using cars, and so they vote for politicians who respond to their interest in traffic flows, road widths and parking. It is mostly only in cities that were impossible to reengineer or where people can't afford cars that we have had pro-cycling mayors like Boris Johnson (London) or Enrique Peñalosa (Bogotá). Most cities, though, are more like this one pictured here in Australia (Launceston), where a simple Nolli map exercise is enough to show clearly the voting power of drivers and the political powerlessness of the risk-averse cyclist. The drivers have most of the contested public space of the city centre to drive in and park on. Risk-averse cyclists are left with some shared footpaths, broken by driveways.

A constructive way forward, now we know cars are destructive, is to give those people who are open to possibilities an alternative vision of bike-centric living. Most first-world cities have the potential for a bicycling layer on land left vacant since manufacturing left; Karl Kullmann refers to webs of 'linear voids' in the post-industrial city.[12] The hope would be to eke out a better existence on the bike layers than can be matched across the rest of the city where cars are the norm, and trust the bike layers thrive and become models for city expansion. They might even inspire some remediation of CBDs that have cars, and inspire whole new cities in the developing world. Before we can get to that point, though, we need to ask if a bike city or layer can possibly trump the car-focused city in terms of convenience.

Despite being expensive, polluting and bad for our waistlines, a city designed around cars does set a high bar when it comes to convenience. Picture a mother minding a baby that is due for a nap, but the mother needs to go shopping and would also like to go for a run for some exercise – and let us suppose it is likely to rain. In a car city she can put her baby to sleep in a car seat and transfer that seat between her car, shopping trolley and a jogging pram if it's not raining when she gets to the park. Missions like these get easier with every decade as the production of car-space becomes more refined and as the designed world adapts around driving.

Nevertheless, the competitive advantage of the box bike means a city designed especially for cycling could in fact make our mother's mission more pleasant. Give her a box bike with retractable casters and she could use it as a grocery trolley inside supermarkets. Design the lifts and corridors of her apartment building so she can ride her box bike all the way to her apartment and she would be able to unpack her groceries directly into her pantry.

Next, design the space between her apartment and the supermarket to quarantine her and her baby from motorized vehicles and give it the kinds of undulations an architect might design if reliving that euphoric moment when he or she first learned to ride. Our hypothetical mother could be getting her exercise, and having fun, on her way home with the shopping. We needn't worry about the baby getting plenty of sleep. Anyone who has ever laid a child down in a box bike will know these bikes are nature's Phenergan.

Supermarkets and malls would not need very much tweaking for box bikes to be ridden inside. Retailers would just need convincing that bikes

11
See: Catherine Lutz and Anne Lutz Fernandez, Carjacked: The Culture of the Automobile and Its Effect on Our Lives (Basingstoke: Palgrave Macmillan, 2010).

12
Karl Kullmann, 'Green-Networks: Integrating Alternative Circulation Systems into Post-industrial Cities', Journal of Urban Design, Vol. 18 (2013) No. 1, 36-58.

13
The arguments for trying to build healthy environments are well documented. For example see: Andrew Dannenberg, Howard Frumkin and Richard Jackson (Eds.) *Making Healthy Places: Designing and Building for Health, Well-being, and Sustainability* (Washington: Island Press, 2011). The difficulty such authors have is in prescribing designs that will literally function to elevate Metabolic Equivalent of Task (MET) rates to useful levels for fitness. The only things in the built environment that can reliably do that are stairs and bike paths, if they are used. Short of calls to make these 'attractive' previous thinkers on this topic have come up with surprisingly little in the way of real advice.

are not horses and aren't about to crap on the floor – the silent steed has been punished for too long for the bad habits of its predecessor.

The apartment building is the greater architectural challenge. With its present reliance on small lifts and stairs, it makes leaving home on your bike about as natural as washing your hands used to be when leaving the toilet, prior the advent of basins in houses. In the olden days, bothering with hand washing was only for those who were as paranoid about infectious disease as you need to be paranoid these days, about chronic disease, to bother with cycling.

A century ago building design changed to incentivize hand washing, an event that reduced rates of infectious disease and thus increased lifespans. The present century could witness building design changed to incentivize cycling. That would reduce chronic disease, the killer we still haven't been able to tackle with our architecture or building codes.[13] If we are to change sedentary lifestyles through the way we design buildings, we need to learn a lesson from hand basins and toilets, which is that architecture needs to be habit *creating* to achieve positive outcomes across populations. None of us should have to go looking for a basin as we leave a toilet. The basin should intercept us. Likewise with cycling: buildings should do everything short of putting bikes in our hands and giving us a push on the back to get going.

Bill Dunster was thinking this way when he designed Velocity, a large office proposal with a sloping roof that he envisioned as a site for row housing. Had it been built, residents would have been able to take a lift to the top and ride down the office-block roof to their house. Upon leaving they would have ridden the rest of the way down the roof to the ground. The combination of lifts and ramps would have given people that metaphorical push on the back to get going. Leaving by bike would have been an easier option than leaving on foot or by car. They show how every access gallery or corridor can be ramped.

Conventional slab blocks, as shown here, defer to the slowness of walking with access corridors as short as can be. The wheels we all need to go beyond our immediate neighbourhoods generally can't be taken in lifts so we are forced to go looking for wheels of some kind when we get to the ground. Imagine if the wheels we would use to go to work, our universities, the opera or disco, were as easy to collect when leaving home as our overcoats or our wallets. And imagine if this meant we could leave a building in a matter of seconds, rather than waiting for then riding a lift. That is the promise of convenience made by the slip block.

Some technical details now. Energy-scavenging floor plates could be used to power lights and save cyclists having to brake on their way down. All the propositions in this book work with first-world requirements for wheelchair access that ramp gradients cannot exceed 1:14 between regular landings or 1:20 (3 degrees) without landings.

Since most people would use lifts to go up but not down, one lift could be provided in situations where normally there would be two without impacting waiting times because of the halving. The corollary to a reduction in the number of lifts is that lift carriages could be made larger

Hand washing made hard

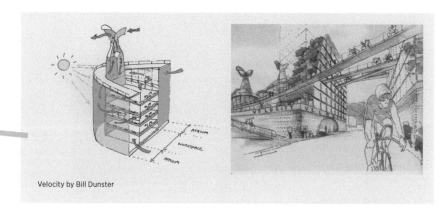

Velocity by Bill Dunster

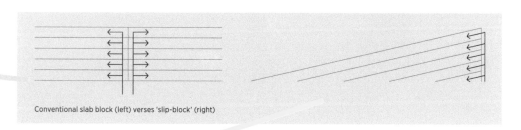

Conventional slab block (left) verses 'slip-block' (right)

Needing fewer lifts mean lifts can be bigger

Visualisation of a 5m wide double-loaded access corridor . . .

Speed humps

Singaporean flats

to accommodate bikes without affecting the overall cost of construction or the cost of lift maintenance.

**Safety Concerns**

Can sloping access galleries, or sloping corridors, be made safe and inviting despite their length and the presence of bikes? Making them wider would be the first step.

Increasing the width of a circulation space may seem extravagant, but not when you consider the cost of parking garages in a building designed around that space-hungry mode. The proposition Unite d' Bicycle Nation for Copenhagen features an internal access corridor just wide enough for a two-way cycle track. Pedestrian paths at the edge would be protected from bicycle traffic by parked bikes at the edge.

You will note in the visualisation how the cycle track is cambered to irritate pedestrians' ankles and how the pedestrian tracks are textured to irritate cyclists. The aim is to protect people on foot from people on bikes while clearing a way for people on bikes.

While no kind of barrier, except actual gates, can guarantee a child will never step in front of a bike, we can reduce the likelihood of such an accident through thoughtful design, and take comfort knowing the consequences would be less dramatic than if a child stepped out of a row house into the path of a car. Likewise, we can't do much as designers to prevent extreme reckless behaviour, except to periodically add speed humps, like the humps used on cycle tracks near schools in the Netherlands, and trust that eventual users will take responsibility for security and for policing.

One of the most effective ways of policing regular ground-level streets is to give residents an incentive to do the policing themselves. People are less inclined to go inside and close their curtains if their own vehicle or their plants are on the same street where they hear a commotion.

If we look at public housing in Singapore we see this also holds true for aerial streets. Nine out of ten Singaporeans live in multistorey public housing blocks with aerial streets – some of them incredibly long – that any member of the public can roam. Authorities allow residents to line these spaces with shoe racks, potted plants, parked bikes and other personal items provided a 1.2 m right of way is preserved.[14] The trade-off to authorities for having to occasionally patrol these spaces to ensure compliance with the 1.2 m rule, is having residents patrol these spaces 24/7 watching over their plants and their bikes. From this we can see that bikes parked in an aerial street could do more than just buffer pedestrians from people on bikes. They could encourage passive surveillance.

Passive surveillance within Singaporean flat blocks benefits from a determination of the Housing and Development Board (HDB) that smoke crossing an access gallery to the outdoors from the window of an apartment does not obstruct egress via that gallery. Some other building codes treat apartments as fire sources that have to be separated from common areas with fireproof doors and solid walls. Often, that means no windows.

Is it inevitable that access ways, if residents can't look upon them, will become sites of more crime? Many assume so, because a period of mismanagement of high-density housing blocks, when they were in the hands of public-housing authorities, happens to have coincided with a

14
'Fire Safety Guidelines For HDB Estates, Guidelines on Usage of Common Corridor', available online: http://www.nfec.gov.sg/firePg_HDB_guidelines.html, accessed 2 May 2014. Thanks to the Love Cycling Singapore group, and especially Eugene Tan for responding to my query about this issue via their Facebook community page.

15
Charles Jencks, *The
Language of Post-Modern
Architecture*, (London:
Academy Editions,
[1977]), 9-10.

16
Katherine Bristo, 'The
Pruitt-Igoe Myth', *JAE*,
Vol. 44 (May 1991) No. 3,
163-171.

17
'Afdeling 4.5. Buiten-
berging, nieuwbouw,
bouwbesluit', available
online: http://www.bou-
wbesluitonline.nl/Inhoud/
docs/wet/bb2012/hfd4/
afd4-5.

proliferation of blind aerial streets inspired by the ones in Le Corbusier's Unité d'habitation. With his lectures and writings on the death of modernism, Charles Jencks has us believe that architecture was the sole cause of social-housing disasters like Pruitt-Igoe.[15] However, that hypothesis has since been dispelled as a myth.[16] Unemployment and government neglect were the prime cause of the fecklessness and the muggings. The architectural setting was just an additional source of aggravation.

What lesson should we really be taking from this? It should not be to rule out long-access ways in apartments, especially when they could help us incentivize bike use. The lesson should be to spend design time, and money, mitigating known problems.

It is possible to put eyes on an access corridor with fire rated glass panels that give residents an outlook onto this space. Corridors can also have communal spaces along them – workshops, yoga rooms, meeting rooms, clothes drying spaces, playground equipment, etcetera – to encourage civilized use. Fire and smoke screens can be fitted to the outside of operable windows. The added costs are worth bearing if they mean incentives can be built in to ride bikes, be healthy, eliminate congestion, reduce greenhouse emissions and improve the lives of people, especially parents with children, who might otherwise leave the city to live in the suburbs where they would have internal garages.

### Bikes Within the Secure Confines of the Apartment

Still, parents' lives won't be as easy as parents' in car land if we don't make space for their bikes within the secure confines of their apartment. It is assumed with the plans accompanying these propositions that the natural place to keep peoples' bikes, if the aim is to encourage bike trips (the way basins encourage hand washing), is immediately inside the apartment. The common practice of storing bikes out on balconies makes people backtrack when leaving. The practice of storing bikes in common areas, while it may encourage passive surveillance, should really only be thought of as a means of providing spill-over bike parking.

There is no substitute for bike storage behind a locked door with secure access to the apartment. It allows people to keep their wallets, purses, sunglasses and keys in their panniers and never have to remove these bags from their bikes. Anything less would deprive urban cyclists of a convenience that people take for granted in car land.

The advertisements posted by American project-home builders of their standard plans leave us in little doubt as to how Americans moving to new suburbs want their vehicles integrated into their homes. They want to keep them under the roofs beneath which they sleep, behind the same lockable doors and have internal access to their kitchens for bringing in groceries.

It is worth pausing to ask why families moving into new houses on the outskirts of Dutch cities, where most shopping trips are done using bikes, have not pushed that country's builders and architects to provide an equivalent level of amenity in bicycle parking. The building code of the Netherlands mandates the provision of bike-storage rooms but doesn't actually specify that these require indoor access to kitchens.[17] The code focuses instead on bike rooms having access to roads and not having windows, lest they be converted to be used as habitable spaces. It is not

Unite de Habitation Le Corbusier

Pruitt Igoe acces corridor

Bike accessible gallery. Designer: Rob Jetson

New row housing in Nijmegen Noord

18
For an example of a developer's plan advertising indoor bike parking as a sale feature in a Dutch home see: 'Cycling and Choosing a Place to Live', *Bicycle Dutch*. Available online: https://bicycledutch.wordpress.com/2011/09/22/cycling-and-chosing-a-place-to-live/, accessed 26 March 2015.

19
Shirley Agudo, *The Dutch and Their Bikes: Scenes from a Nation of Cyclists*, (Schiedam: XPat Scriptum Publishers, 2014).

always the case,[18] but what typically results in new Dutch housing estates are lockable bike rooms of the minimum permissible size, next to the laneway, but away from the house.

Are the contexts so different between the Netherlands and the U.S. that internal access from garages (regardless of whether they are built to house motorized vehicles or bicycles) is important in one place but not in the other? The American context may be more indulgent, but still it has people unloading groceries from the machines they used to go shopping.

It would be nice to think home buyers in the Netherlands were pushing architects in this direction, albeit slowly. Unfortunately, the opposite seems to be true. When the section of the building code requiring bike rooms was temporarily dropped in 2003 during a nine-year period when Dutch legislators hoped they could trust the housing market to self-regulate, bike storage rooms disappeared altogether. The average buyer was apparently happy enough to chain their bike to a street pole.

Now that the law has been reintroduced, the most common response is still to build bike rooms separated from houses by courtyards. In row housing contexts people can get around this by rolling their bikes into their kitchens. However, compared to Americans in car suburbs they would face a significant number of impositions: having to wheel their bikes back to bike sheds after unpacking their groceries; having to wheel bikes that might have snow on the wheels across carpet; or, out of laziness, finding they often park their bikes inside, but in inconvenient places. Americans who have witnessed developers responding to ever-greater market demands might be surprised by Dutch home buyers' acceptance of house plans that offer little more convenience than plans from past eras.

Could the hardy Dutch national character be a factor at play? Without it the Dutch might not have persisted with cycling when other nationalities were turning to driving. But if only the Dutch were a little more lazy! They might have spent their century with bikes doing what Americans have done during their half-century living with cars: eliminating inconveniences by fine tuning the design of their housing to harmonize with their main mode of transport.

A recent picture book, *The Dutch & Their Bikes*,[19] celebrates the way a Dutch woman will cheerily lift her bike onto a train. A designer would be asking why the train floor is not the same height as the platform. Other photos show people happily riding in the rain or the snow. If Americans had cycling as their preferred mode, and had spent money on bike infrastructure the way they spend money on freeways, their bike paths would all have glass covers by now and snow-melting elements under the asphalt.

Designers should know what they are risking by designing for a sector of the Dutch population that is too easily pleased. The Dutch national character could change with the next generation, or wave of immigration, and with that new governments could be elected with policies that favour the lily-livered over the hardy. Roads could be widened for cars and farmland released for American style subdivisions. Developing optimal cycling environments that provide more convenience than driving environments is one way the current generation can insulate their country against these possibilities.

Optimizing buildings for bicycle use would also make good business sense for this nation that profits by exporting its knowledge. The Netherlands has a reputation for architectural innovation traceable all the way back to De Stijl. The reflected and direct glory gives almost any Dutch firm a head start when it comes to winning international work. The same goes for Dutch bike planning and mobility consultancies whose international markets have been greatly expanding as the rest of the world wakes up to the benefits of urban cycling.

By combining their talents, Dutch architects and bicycling experts could approach their own country's new housing as a test-bed for real innovation. Many of the bicycling experts, though, would need to have it explained that the new design measures would not be targeting concerns as they see them. Too many bicycling experts are drawn from the ranks of proud cyclists. They wear inconvenience as a demonstrative hair shirt. People of this personality type in the Netherlands relish the rain and admonish fair-weather cyclists for making excuses. In car-centric nations they relish riding in traffic and admonish non-cyclists for their lack of fitness and overblown perceptions of danger. Proud cyclists are the mortal enemy of environmental design aimed at getting more people cycling.

It makes no sense pitching new design measures at avid cyclists whose enjoyment and pride is derived from environments that are poorly designed. As designers we need to be pleasing the occasional cyclist, whose commitment could easily wane. These could include new parents who we know cycle less during this stage of life.[20] They could be the baby boomers who are cycling a lot at the moment, but will need less challenging environments if they are to continue cycling into their eighties.[21] Or they could belong to immigrant populations who are underrepresented in cycling participation statistics.[22] When Dutch architects can provide a house-and-bike package so comfortable that even senior citizens, new parents and immigrants stop being swayed by the American house-and-car package, they will have invented something they can export.[23]

## Caring for Bikes Means Caring for People

If we take a slightly longer historical view, we see the Netherlands is not the only nation where residential housing designers have given the bike perfunctory treatment. Bicycling was a mainstay for commuters in the U.K. for the first half of the twentieth century, but when future archaeologists sift through the ruins of London what evidence of that will they find?[24] There will be nothing to compare to the footings of tram sheds or buried steel train lines, or any equivalents of the stone horse troughs kept now to grow plants in, or the millions of stairs testifying to the perennial importance of walking.

All those artefacts put together won't hold a candle to the thousands of ruined garages. So many parking garages await archaeologists that future generations might wonder if cars weren't the dominant species and humans weren't slaves kept to drive them. As for evidence of England's reliance on bikes, there may well be nothing at all.

This should lead us away from asking why the Dutch treat their bikes with no love and instead to asking what it is about bikes that makes

20
Eva Heinen, *Bicycle Commuting* (Delft: Delft University Press, 2011).

21
Lucas Harms, Luca Bertolini and Marco Brömmelstroet, 'Social and Spatial Differentiation of Bicycle Use Patterns in the Netherlands, *Proceedings of the 13th WCTR*, 15-18 July 2013, Rio de Janeiro.

22
According to the Dutch Cycling Embassy, the growth of suburban-based immigrant populations in the west of the Netherlands and an ageing population are impacting the national bike modal share. See online: http://www.fietsberaad.nl/index.cfm?lang=nl&repository=Fietsberaad+-publicatie+11b.+Het+effect+van+de+toe-name+van+het+aantal+allochtonen+en+de+vergri-jzing+op+het+fietsgebruik, accessed 15 May 2014.

23
The Dutch Cycling Embassy has also identified Moroccan and Turkish as groups who are least likely to cycle. See online: http://www.fietsberaad.nl/index.cfm?lang=nl&repository=Fietsberaad+-publicatie+11a.+Het+fietsgebruik+van+allochtonen+nader+belicht, accessed 15 May 2014.

24
Colin Pooley and Jean Turnbull, 'Modal Choice and Modal Change: The Journey to Work in Britain since 1890, *Journal of Transport Geography*, Vol. 8 (2000) No. 1, 11-24.

25
Filippo Tommaso Marinetti, 'Futurist Manifestor', in: R.W. Flint (Ed.), *Marinetti: Selected Writings* (New York: Farrar, Straus and Giroux, 1972), 39-44. First published in *Le Figaro* (20 February 1909).

26
Roland Barthes, *Mythologies: The Complete Edition, in a New Translation*, translated by Annette Lavers and Richard Howard (New York: Farrar, Straus and Giroux, 2013).

27
Nikolaus Pevsner, *An Outline of European Architecture*, 6th edition (Harmondsworth: Penguin Books, 1960), 7.

28
http://architecturefor-dogs.com/, accessed 21 May 2014.

them so unlovable. Why have bicycles had so little impact on the building stock of all nations? Bikes do not kick with hind legs like the horses our ancestors built glorious stables to house. They don't leak oil from sumps like the cars we garage. Neither do they cram us into tight spaces like the trains and planes we glorify with awe inspiring stations and airports. So why doesn't the built environment glorify bikes? The truth is, it did, but for too short a time for our bike love to take root in any ongoing way in architectural practice. The bicycle had only been enthralling us for a decade when it was eclipsed by the car.

No story illustrates the bike's penumbral relationship to the car more aptly than that of Horace Dobbins's ill-fated California Cycleway. Opened in 1900 as an elevated bicycle tollway from Pasadena, and planned to extend the whole 16 km to Los Angeles, it was demolished before the end of the decade, its route later built over by the Pasadena Freeway (now Arroyo Seco Parkway) for cars.

Infrastructure and building projects for cars captured the public's imagination as perhaps no building works for the bike ever will. But if you think cloverleaf freeways and parking garages indicate the limits of car love, pause to consider the lyrical waxing that has been bestowed on cars themselves. They have graced the world with a new beauty, the beauty of speed, wrote Filippo Marinetti in 1909.[25] They are almost the exact equivalent of Gothic cathedrals, wrote Roland Barthes in 1957.[26] Three years later the leading architectural historian of the mid-twentieth century, Nicholas Pevsner, was saying bike sheds proved that not every building is architecture the way Lincoln Cathedral is architecture.[27] We take it for granted that Pevsner picked on the bike shed and not the car-parking garage.

All this praise surrounding the car, and inauspiciousness surrounding the bike, means architects who care about their discipline's hermetic concerns really have no inclination toward bicycle parking. It's not the kind of thing that will bring them peer recognition. If fame and awards are their goal, their time would actually be better spent designing dog kennels; a project called *Architecture for Dogs* has brought together Toyo Ito, Atelier Bow-Wow, Kazuyo Sejima, MVRDV, Shigeru Ban and other big names for the edification of bourgeois bichons.[28]

When we consider the hurdles cities are facing with chronic disease, gridlock and greenhouse emissions it is a shame no similar group of famous architects has brought the same sense of a fun challenge to the design of bicycle parking as this group has brought to dog kennels. This is no laughing matter. Architects really are underperforming across social fronts. More attention is paid to their canon of cathedrals – be they stone ones in Lincoln, cars, or the museum in Bilbao – than to the social agenda upon which modernism was originally founded.

The tendency among architects to judge one another using terms of reference drawn from their discipline's canon can be understood through the lens of Jacques Rancière's critique of something he calls the 'representational regime of art'. Beyond his peculiar jargon and the unfortunate translations from French lies a cutting critique of artists who work in the service of their peers, reaffirming normative definitions of what their art is, and is not, without really serving the masses.

California cycleway

Architecture for. . . dogs?

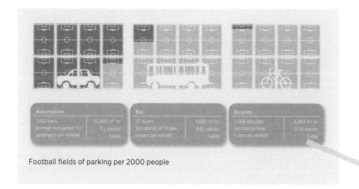

Football fields of parking per 2000 people

From Proposition 2, page 85

29
Jacques Ranciere, *The Politics of Aesthetics: The Distribution of the Sensible*, translated by Gabriel Rockhill (London: Continuum, 2004).

30
ASCOBIKE + ITDP, *Bicycle Parking Facility Manual*, diagram from page 17. Available online: https:// go.itdp.org/display/live/ Bicycle+Parking+Facility +Manual, accessed 6 May 2014.

Unlike most art theorists, whose ideas are shaped by aesthetic philosophies, Rancière looks at artists' work from the standpoint of labour theory. Reading his key text on art, *The Politics of Aesthetics*, opens our minds to a question that cuts across style: 'Who are architects working to please?'[29] It might be other architects, as mentioned already. Alternatively, if they work to reinforce ideologies – capitalism, monarchy, religion, etcetera – Rancière says they are working according to the 'ethical regime of art'. If they are serving the masses and not stealing away from them when they could be engaging as real collaborators, Rancière says they are working within the 'aesthetic regime of art', the regime he views as authentic and which he says is most clearly seen in Russian constructivism. He is not saying architecture should *look* constructivist (the very fact that qualification needs to be made shows how deeply lost we are in the 'representational regime'). Rather, he wants architects, and artists generally, to work in the manner of the constructivists, *with* the masses, toward their liberation. Given his support of the 1968 student riots in Paris, Rancière would see liberating the masses from their current dependence on oil and car companies as about the most vital, or 'Rancièrian' mission an architect could ever embark on.

We are not just considering the space between buildings and how architects can make them bike friendly. We are thinking of buildings themselves and what architects can do to make them natural generators and receptors of bike trips. The best work of bike network planners, connecting safe routes like lengths of brass plumbing, is being undone at the ends. In terms plumbing analogies, it is helpful to think of an apartment building as something akin to a reservoir. Flows throughout entire networks are weakened if reservoirs are leaky or clogged. Reservoirs of people's bikes in their apartment complexes are leaky if they don't protect a city's bicycle fleet from vandals or thieves, and clogged if they don't make leaving home on a bike as simple as letting water flow into a pipe from a dam.

The best way of protecting populations from bicycle theft is by enabling people to keep their daily-use bikes within the secure confines of their abodes. How much space should be provided? We won't know for sure until life and the way we design has been given a few decades to settle down around the kinds of purpose-built bicycling districts that right now we can only imagine. Should we be worried if bike storage spaces as large as garages became a feature of apartment designs in the future? Considering the vulgar size of car parks and the compactness of bicycle parking (measured in soccer fields in the infographic from Brazil), it would cost us all less to store venerable collections of bikes in our flats than we currently pay to build basement garages for one or two cars.[30]

If we take a broad view we see the conventional slab block gets its form from the slowness of walking, a mode that demands the shortest possible distances between apartment doors and lift-banks. The slip block prioritises the needs of people with bikes. A cyclist would not be so bothered by the length of a gallery since they could shorten that length, time wise, by just letting go of their brakes. A cyclist could exit their apartment and be out of a slip block in a fraction of the time it takes pedestrians in a conventional slab block to walk from their apartments and ride lifts to the ground. Better still, cyclists would reach the ground equipped with a vehicle, something a driver would have to collect from a basement garage.

Like the first proposition for New York, this one for 'the city of cyclists' isn't being shown with the gardens and community paces that would organically gather at its base, since there wouldn't be cars there. The graphic intension is to shock in the manner of Le Corbusier's Plan Voisin, while at the same time highlighting the salient features of a new architecture that can be teleologically traced to the unique characteristics of bicycle motion.

## Proposition 3:
## Alexandria Apartments and Cyclelogistics Centre in Sydney

The third proposition centres on the idea of stacking slip blocks that can be taller than the ones shown in the Copenhagen example without being so long. Another way to understand the ramps is to imagine a hillside village organized around a switchback trail with lanes feeding from it, like the ancient Greek city of Delphi. Now imagine Delphi being compressed horizontally until the switchback trail is scaling a near vertical cliff.

One oversized lift at the end of the block takes people on bikes to their sloping floor level. From the lift they ride down their ramped access gallery to their apartment. When leaving, it would be faster to roll down to the ground than bothering using the lift.

Issues arising for discussion include the problem of two-storey apartments with aging populations, cultural prejudices about aerial streets and resonances between this and failed public-housing estates from the 1960s.

### Two-Storey Dwellings
It is not essential for scissored, slipped, helical or multi-helical apartment block types to include double-storey apartments. A helix of single-storey dwelling units would likely work well as student or elderly housing.

Single-storey apartments are almost essential for disabled users and single-person households, and they are preferred by older buyers who anticipate having trouble with stairs in coming years. Their problem is they rely on machines. If the aim is to design each unit with private windows on two or more sides, then they have to be paired around lift cores. Building managers are left with a lot of lifts to maintain and therefore a big bill to pass on to tenants or owners. The number of lifts can be reduced with longer access galleries, but to avoid privacy problems this usually means a wall with no windows facing the noise source. How do you cool an apartment with windows on only one side and therefore no cross-ventilation? Typically, with air conditioners. How do you heat an apartment with windows on only one side and therefore less sun penetration? Typically with more heating. Families and cohabiting groups of able bodied people deserve a greater supply of two-storey apartments, without all these compensatory machines.

Delphi

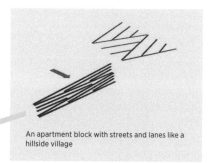

An apartment block with streets and lanes like a hillside village

From Proposition 3, page 120

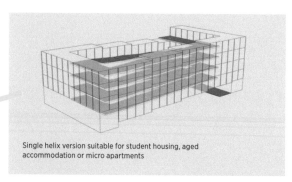

Single helix version suitable for student housing, aged accommodation or micro apartments

Robin Hood Gardens, Peter and Alison Smithson

Traction gained in the past 30 years by champions of simple living, work-life balance, low carbon footprints, etcetera, means we (the educated urban elite, as our detractors might call us) don't want our lives cluttered with gadgets. Our sensibilities allow for a few all-in-one white goods, a Wi-Fi transmitter, an electric toothbrush perhaps, plenty of small transmitting devices and maybe five or six mechanical things that plug in. However, if that list blew out to include treadmills and step climbers in our living rooms, garbage disposal units and soda-water taps at our sinks, spa jets in our bathtubs, hydraulics in our beds, massaging sofas, bidets and heating controls on our toilets and ductwork for our vacuum cleaners, we might not feel as though our homes were our own. They would feel more like those 'homes of the future' our parents dreamed about in the 1950s and 1960s. John Maeda speaks for our generation with *The Laws of Simplicity*, a plea for reduced functionality from all our machines, for sanity's sake.[31]

It is disappointing that a similar curatorial restraint to that shown by city dwellers when deciding what machines are allowed to invade their apartments is not also exhibited by the architects who design the apartments themselves. As we have seen with the new apartment-block types discussed in this book, our dependence on one kind of machine, the passenger lift, can be reduced – or even done away with entirely – if buildings are arranged around access ways that ramp to the ground. The wheels, brakes and transmissions of bicycles would take over the duty of winching and lowering us between the ground and our homes in the air. Once on the ground, the bike would replace the car or the train for cross-city transport. One simple machine that is good for our health would replace two or three complex machines that leave our bodies inactive.

### The Return of the Aerial Street

Architects Peter and Alison Smithson accomplished a lot with Robin Hood Gardens: bedrooms cantilevered out over the access galleries so people sleeping would not be disturbed; natural cooling by cross-venti-lation; natural heating with windows facing the sun; access ways on the outside of the building where they would enjoy fresh air and daylight; and a remarkable ratio of habitable floor space to circulation space given the generous width of those galleries. They were wide enough for the Smithsons to promote them as 'aerial streets'.

In this regard the Smithsons truly believed their access galleries fulfilled a promise made by their hero Le Corbusier to extend the city and its streets into the sky, with the worst things about the ground left behind and the best things replicated nearer the sun and fresh-air streams. In the context of a discussion of bike-centric buildings it has to be mentioned that some copies of Le Corbusier's 1923 book *Vers une architecture*,[32] with its aerial street on the cover, had an alternative photo with a cyclist shown riding the length of that street.

In the case of Le Corbusier's works and the Smithsons', the term 'aerial street' should be used reservedly. These are not streets like the ones we stumble upon when we walk or ride about exploring networks of regular streets on the ground. Unless we venture into a lift or a staircase, we will never find them. No wonder they feel so foreboding! They should

31
John Maeda, *The Laws of Simplicity (Simplicity: Design, Technology, Business, Life)* (Cambridge, MA: MIT Press, 2006).

32
Le Corbusier, *Vers une architcture* (Paris: Les éditions G. Crès, 1923).

33
Space Syntax is a method
devised by Bill Hillier
and Julienne Hanson
for analysing spatial
relationships in buildings
and cities in an abstract
and mathematical manner,
in isolation from questions
of style. See: Bill Hillier
and Julienne Hanson,
*The Social Logic of Space*
(Cambridge: Cambridge
University Press, 1984).

34
Steven Fleming (video
clip), 'Architecture for
Bicycles in Copenhagen'
(1 July 2011). Available
online: https://www.
youtube.com/watch?v=-
q-e9_KFcoY, accessed
12 October 2014.

be called 'aerial alleys' in acknowledgement of their actual space syntax relationship to the rest of the streets in the city.[33]

The aerial streets of BIG's 8 House in Copenhagen (2010) are far more like regular streets. Simply by making them sloping, the architects have made these galleries possible to stumble upon without entering lifts or walking up stairs. They quite simply grow out of the street on the ground.

One deficiency of the 8 House – that the propositions in this book would overcome – is that only around half of its apartments are accessed via those aerial streets. Most are reached via lifts serving as few as two apartments per level. Another is that it wasn't really conceived as a bike access building. In 2011, BIG's press office recommended it to me as a bike access building. In July 2011, I filmed myself cycling down the aerial streets.[34] However, by the passing of the next winter, signs had appeared prohibiting cycling. In saving on the height and the strength of their balustrades, and by not building heating elements into the pavement to melt ice and snow, the architects forsook an opportunity to realize Le Corbusier's vision on the cover of *Vers une architecture* that shows a cyclist riding along an aerial street.

A giant housing block in Chengdu, China by Jiakun Architects, called the West Village Basis Yard, brings us much closer to a future when cycling to the street from your high-level flat will be normal. Finished in 2014, this colossal u-shaped perimeter block is closed on the fourth side by a concertina of ramps that ultimately connect all the access galleries to each other, the ground and the roof. Promotional photographs showing a group of cyclists touring the roof, and scale models of cyclists on the model of the project at the 2016 Venice Biennale, leave no doubt that the architects intended the building to be used in this way.

### Positioning Velotopia

There are two more ways apartments can be designed so that cyclists can ride all the way to the ground. One is to arrange floor plates horizontally, in the conventional manner, but to slice those floor plates with an inclined roof that doubles as a ramp to the ground. Although bike egress was not at the forefront of his thinking, Friedensreich Hundertwasser designed his Waldspirale apartments with access corridors leading onto a green roof in this way. The roof provides a nature walk (or nature ride) to the ground as an alternative to an elevator or stairs.

Another way of bringing bikes to higher levels is by letting the site do the ramping. This can only be done on sloping sites, that are less likely to be developed with a bicycling focus. Nevertheless, opportunities will sometimes be found to use topography to gain high-level access to multi-storey blocks of apartments, as has been done in the past.

One example is Affonso Eduardo Reidy's seven-storey Pedregulho Housing Complex experiment in Rio de Janeiro (1947-1952). Because it is on the low side of the road and on a very steep hillside, access is via a bridge to the third level. This level is void and used solely for horizontal circulation to stairs that take residents up or down to their apartments. Naturally the void deck is ridden on, not only by cyclists, but motorcyclists as well. The building is, after all, in one of the world's hilliest cities and one that has very few controls on where motorbikes are allowed to be ridden.

8-house aerial street

West Basis Yard, Liu Jiakun Architects

Cyclist in the Rain and the Waldspirale, by Friedensreich Hundertwasser

Pedregulho Housing experiment

Mountian bikers hotel

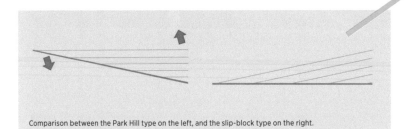

Comparison between the Park Hill type on the left, and the slip-block type on the right.

Park Hill Estate

A well-publicized student proposal from 2010 for a hotel to serve mountain-bike riders would have used a similar strategy, in this case to ensure that every level could be reached on a bike.

Another project where the terrain provides on-grade access to upper levels is Park Hill Estate in Sheffield, England (1957-1961) by Jack Lynn and Ivor Smith. This project provides the perfect note on which to end our discussion of housing for the way it leads our minds back to the slip block. If the buildings of Park Hill Estate could be picked up and dropped on a flat site, they would almost be slip blocks.

Just like the milk floats that once roamed these galleries, cyclists can travel horizontally until the level plane of their floors intersect the rising plane of the hillside below, and that way reach the ground without having to use the stairs or the lift. Whether they lived in a slip block on a flat site, or at Park Hill Estate, the distance required to travel along an aerial street would be longer the higher a person lived from the ground. The disadvantage to a cyclist of an address in Park Hill Estate is they would not have gravity to make their aerial-street ride to the ground quite as tempting as it would be if they lived in a slip block. They might be tempted instead to leave their bike at home and walk to the lift.

We know what populations without bikes tend to do when discharged onto streets. They converge upon transit nodes where retailers concentrate shops. Streets en route to those nodes brim with commerce but steal people and their watchful eyes from the rest of the city, leaving most parts with no passive surveillance. Other people leaving home without bikes might choose to leave via basement garages, in which case they directly do damage to streets, turning them into places of congestion, pollution and regular tragedy. The apartment types we have looked at in this book would have a positive impact on any urban environment, especially ones designed in anticipation of cycling. The only niggling concern is that neo-brutalist mega-blocks carry too much of a stigma, still. Ben Wheatley's 2015 film adaptation of J.G. Ballard's *High-Rise* (1975) shows audiences are as ready as ever to believe a building can push its residents toward tribal violence.[35] Are such fears real or imagined? Residents of Liu Jiakun's West Village Basis Yard in Chengdu would never understand all the fuss.

This is not to deny mistakes of the past. For example, Chalkhill Estate in the Wembley Park area of northwest London had to be demolished in 2000 after decades of stigma and crime. It was almost a direct copy of the Park Hill Estate as well! And who could ignore the Ballardian chaos that went on at the Hulme Crescents until it was demolished in 1994? But neither event spelt the end for mega-blocks generally, or for the aerial street. The Park Hill Estate is still standing. Not only that, it has heritage listing: it's the largest listed building in Europe. It has also undergone a complete renovation and is in the process of being sold off to yuppies.

The lesson of Park Hill Estate's survival is that Le Corbusier, Peter and Alison Smithson and the lesser known architects who were in the process of refining these large building types with aerial streets were wrongly made into scapegoats. Bulldozing working-class neighbour-

35
Ben Child, 'Ben Wheatley to Direct Adaptation of JG Ballard's High Rise [sic]', The Guardian (30 August 2013). Available online: http://www.theguardian.com/film/2013/aug/29/ben-wheatley-jg-ballard-high-rise, accessed 3 April 2014.

36
For a great collection
of photos from the time
when Manhattan's lots had
freestanding houses see:
Hilary Ballon (Ed.), *The
Greatest Grid: The Master
Plan of Manhattan,* 1811-
2011 (New York: Columbia
University Press, 2012).

hoods to manufacture new ones further out from the city will wreak havoc no matter what form the buildings of the new district might take. And if inventive architects from the past can't really be blamed for ruining lives, we should not be strayed from our mission of making lives better through more invention. Economies of scale make big buildings cheaper to build. This is good for the poor and good for cities that otherwise push the poor to the outskirts, thus turning city centres into middle-class ghettos. As developments go up in size, the relative cost of energy-saving systems comes down, for example systems that draw heat from the sewer or gather wind power. Aerial streets reduce the ratio of lifts to apartments, sharing lift-maintenance costs between many residents instead of a few. Two-storey apartments keep a reign on the relative size of those aerial streets while enhancing cross-ventilation, privacy and access to sunlight.

The next step in the mega-block renaissance, which started with BIG's 8 House, is to correct the space syntax of the aerial street. At the same time we need to make aerial streets incentives to leave home via bike, the mode topping the scales across all three major fronts: health, sustainability and speed of connection for the whole city. The aerial street needs to tilt to the ground.

## Proposition 4:
## Newcastle Waterway Discovery Loop

For every city with millions of people that we have all heard of, there are a hundred third- and fourth-tier cities that interest nobody except those who live there, with populations anywhere between 100,000 and 500,000. That notwithstanding, the shift we are seeing toward a planet of city dwellers, is more a product of 4,000 small cities doubling or tripling than a few dozen big cities growing by a half or one third. Newcastle is not a mega city right now. That's why it's of interest.

Small cities with cars are like young adults eating snack foods. Young people can't see the day coming when their habit will have clogged their arteries. People who live in small cities can't see how their habit of driving will soon clog their roads.

If they could see, they would start rezoning land in annular waves radiating out from the centre. Every homeowner could replace their freestanding house with 20 New York or Parisian style flats on the same block of land, built to the side and front boundaries. Four per level. Five storeys high. Few elevators and no parking at all. There are old photos of freestanding houses across upper Manhattan that explain the transition.[36] In time, each of Manhattan's houses was demolished and replaced with a solid lump of walk-up apartments. They were living in fortunate times. Back then they didn't have NYMBYs touting garden-city clichés to restrict the supply of centrally located housing.

In cities where the inner suburbs can't grow thicker or higher, urban consolidation is relying on the dense redevelopment of docklands, contaminated wastelands, logistics lands, and other such land that we don't need as much of in the post-industrial era. The proposition for Newcastle

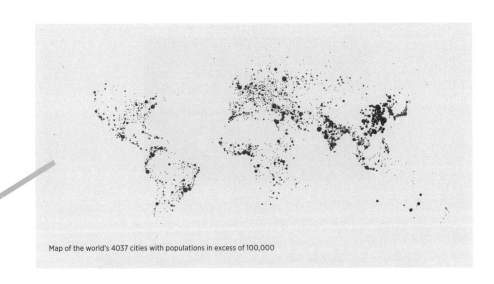

Map of the world's 4037 cities with populations in excess of 100,000

View South from Park Avenue and 94th Street, Manhattan

A view from the roof of a home at Park Avenue and 94th Street from around 1882-1883

The selfishness of restricting density

Space in Newcastle that drivers don't see

The Newcastle waterway discovery loop

Glass clad automated storage and retrieval systems for bikes

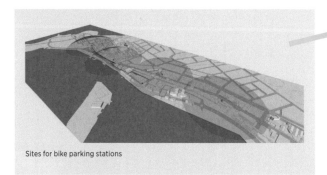

Sites for bike parking stations

starts with a crude mapping of that land, plus parkland and non-vehicular easements where cycling would not bother voters who drive.

Where amidst all the blue on that map could a linear park or green loop project be found? The Indianapolis Cultural Trail is a good example of bike infrastructure sold to the car-loving masses as a new and fun way to discover the city's cultural attractions.[37] Another precedent to think of is the Atlanta BeltLine, a popular rail-trail and linear park that has been catalysing redevelopment projects on all the old brownfields it cuts through.[38] Indianapolis and Atlanta aren't places where average tax payers want to see money spent just to please cycling enthusiasts, and neither is Newcastle, Australia.

The proposal is for a linear park project that every tax payer can enjoy for the opportunity it provides to walk or cycle a 7-km loop, seeing their city from a new angle and understanding the flow of the creeks. Existing cyclists would appreciate the way the loop ties together the three major bike routes that stop short of the city. More important still are the large sites coloured yellow on the map that, if they were to be Velotopian, could help populate the city with people choosing bikes for their transport.

Broadmeadow station is the natural departure point for train trips to Sydney. As Newcastle becomes more of a cycling city this station would require something like the rapid-access bike parking facilities now being built under the central train stations of every Dutch city. As a way of celebrating cycling in a city that has neglected it for so long, a less efficient, but glamorous automated storage and retrieval system (ASRS), clad in glass, might have some symbolic worth too.

Indeed, ASRS facilities could celebrate and help cycling in many zones that draw sudden crowds, such as outdoor concert venues, large theatres, beaches in summer and sites of temporary markets, like the site pictured at the beginning of Hunter Street Mall.

Such structures in each of the pictured locations along Hunter Street would serve as beacons to drivers, inviting them to cycle instead, and serve the peak parking needs of this linear strip of crowd-drawing venues and sites.

## Propositions 5, 6, 7 and 8:
## Detroit, Canberra, Brisbane and Amsterdam

Detroit has an abundance of former industrial land, connected by linear voids once used for bulk haulage. It also has houses you can buy for a dollar, and probably redevelop however you like. This is the quintessential post-industrial city. The ratio of land that is fiercely contested by car-driving voters to land with the potential of being redeveloped according to a Velotopian skews so far toward the latter that it could be the boom town of the post-fossil era that it was in the era of cars. There is a real chance that a new development paradigm could attract knowledge-based enterprises to post-industrial cities like these. The bulk haulage routes that once carried commodities to manufacturing plants, would then carry educated minds along bike routes. The opportunities for chance inter-

37
http://indyculturaltrail.org/.

38
http://beltline.org/.

action that cycling affords (how bikes themselves can be conversation starters), could lead many strangers to cafes, to meet and discuss and join forces.

Then there are cities that, in the wake of motordom, have a surplus of ceremonial space. Brasília is the most famous. Canberra is one of the most thinly developed with a population density lower than many of the world's rural areas. The map shows the extent of low-lying ground where future growth could be concentrated and oriented around bicycle transport. On much of it cars would not even need to be banned for bicycles to have the advantage. All that would be needed are pedestrian bridges making cycling the fastest way to cross Lake Burley Griffin.

Before the car and the streetcar, cities expanded most readily on available flat land. Back then it was worth paying to build levees and/or low-friction storm-water canals to win land that could be more easily accessed by trains, boats and horse-drawn carts. In the machine age it became cheaper to run tramlines or roads to high ground. Brisbane is a good example of a city where this phenomenon means vast regions close to the city centre have been relegated to low-value functions because they are flood prone. In the hands of the Dutch the blue space could have become a whole country.

It is not purely a matter of coincidence that the Dutch were building cities in the seventeenth century that would be hard to drive cars on today. City planners back then were still doing something we can see in cities as old as Pompeii: deliberately making streets narrow to limit the flow of carriages into the centre (De Negen Straatjes or 'the nine little streets', for instance). Narrow streets, flatness and a lack of parking (in a centre protected as a UNESCO World Heritage site) have given Amsterdam the most bike-centric centre of any global city since Beijing forsook that particular honour.

There is nothing to guarantee things will stay this way, though. Housing estates in Amsterdam's outer boroughs continue to be built with ample car parking, putting ever more pressure on the centre to let outsiders' cars in. Keen baby-boomer cyclists of Dutch ancestry are leaving for heaven just as groups in the traditionally poor outer boroughs are finding the means to buy mopeds. There aren't a lot of fundamentals to stop Amsterdam losing its cycling tradition and becoming a city of 2-stroke or electric-powered scooters, as safe and attractive as Naples. Recognizing that every new block of housing with car parking provisions tips the scales toward Amsterdam becoming a motorized city is the first step toward recognizing that the reverse is true too. Every new development that is part of a new vision for Amsterdam – car-free and exploiting the possibilities arising when we start to use bikes within buildings – will tip the scales toward cycling.

A 15-km-wide circle centred on Amsterdam Centraal station reveals the importance, to urban expansion, of industrial land in the northwest quadrant and farmland in the north east quadrant. With express routes even slow cyclists could reach the centre from any part of these new 'bike city limits' in 30 minutes.

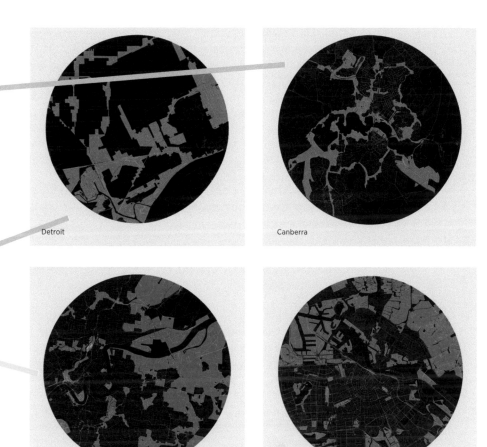

Detroit

Canberra

Brisbane

Amsterdam

Negen straatjes

Pompeii

The world's fastest growing cities

39
Michael John Law, *The Experience of Suburban Modernity: How Private Transport Changed Inter-war London* (Manchester: Manchester University Press, 2014).

40
John Forester, *Effective Cycling* (1976).

As much as Amsterdam would benefit from bike-centric expansion, it could be thousands of other cities, especially in the developing world, that could benefit more. If it embraced a truly bike-centric urban growth model Amsterdam has a chance at dethroning the American car-centric city as the developing world's inspiration. It has a long way to go with its population, needing to grow by roughly 5 times (from 800,000 to 4 million), before it could pique the interest of leaders of cities that grow by the hour. To do that it would need to embrace a ten-fold population density increase; 4,000 people per square kilometre (what they are used to right now) won't let the city grow without sprawling.

There are two bigger hurdles. The second biggest is one the Amsterdammers have already crossed. They understand cycling as a real mode of transport. If that's the second biggest hurdle, what is the biggest? It is having enough faith in bicycle transport to imagine new building types and development patterns that follow the logic of cycling, then only planning for walking and public transport within the new bicycling framework.

## Linear Routes

Inherent to the idea that the metamorphosis of cities could start with demonstration projects is the problem of linking them up. If you think back to the blue-space map of New York and the distances between potential redevelopment sites, it is clear that getting separate bicycle-oriented redevelopment districts to function as a unified whole, a kind of parallel city of value to those of the bicycling lifestyle, could require the construction of some long and lonely greenways bypassing the car-centric districts between.

Before looking at design options for linear routes, the concerns of those who would rather cyclists defend their right to car-centric streets than retreat to what they might see as a layer of last resort need to be answered. Many would understandably argue that dividing communities according to preferred means of transport is like dividing Berlin according to ideology, or Israel and Palestine according to religion, or building gated communities with their own private police to sort the haves from the have-nots. The difference between the segregation informing the bicycle heterotopia plan espoused here, and the kind of segregation that keeps weak and powerful groups apart in some cities, is that neither income or race, or anything else about which people have little control, can force a person to live in the blue space and orient their lives around cycling. It would be their choice, like joining an intentional community.

Even stronger objections to a segregationist approach are likely to come from some bicycle advocates who have always been paranoid about their relegation to the margins. In established urban districts the fear has been that we would lose our right to the middle of the carriageway if cycle paths were provided off to the edge. We see this in the Cyclists' Touring Club of England's opposition to cycle paths as far back as the 1930s,[39] then again in the 1970s when John Forester influenced American road-design policy with his book of tips for staying alive amidst cars.[40]

We know now that when it comes to the street, relegation to the margins can be a great thing for bicycle patronage. Relegation means cyclists at least have a safe space to ride, if not the freedom to turn across traffic as readily as a motorist can. Cycling participation rates have skyrocketed in New York since protected bike lanes were delineated from the carriageway at the edge of some avenues. Participation rates are much higher still in the Netherlands where a bike-conscious traffic-engineering philosophy gives drivers streets with few cyclists and cyclists streets with few drivers. In other words, driving and cycling are largely decoupled. The simple message to take from this is that the more bicycling space is decoupled from driving space, the more cycling thrives.

What is being argued for with these maps, and the bicycling-heterotopias plan more generally, is really just a further decoupling. New districts that have lots of bike parking can exist away from old districts that have lots of car parking. When each way of life has been disentangled and left to thrive or fail on its merits, reason suggests that residents on the side that has lost will be the first ones wanting to bring down the wall and reunite on the winning side's terms.

Now to linear path design, starting with a classic problem seen mainly along waterfront promenades. Pedestrians worry about cyclists bearing down on them from behind while cyclists worry about pedestrians suddenly changing course and stepping into their paths, and everyone except for the designers who keep creating this problem are left with the blame. The usual band-aid solutions include bans on bikes or putting up signs to tell cyclists that they will be blamed for any collision, as though pedestrians were yachts on the harbour and cyclists were speedboats. A somewhat fairer approach, that protects people who regularly walk along linear shared spaces, is to cobble the sides of the path and grind a smooth track down the middle. As pedestrians learn that cobbles bother cyclists more than themselves, they learn that the cobbled edges are for them and the smooth centre is best left for riders. The northern Italian city of Ravenna is a good place to see this approach that is further enhanced by the use of two paving colours. Where it falls down is with tourists who don't know the local code. How then to protect visitor pedestrians from cyclists, and cyclists from them? Curbs, barriers, stencils or signs are common reactions, but all these reduce the conviviality of shared public places. A better way to dissuade pedestrians from paths cyclists need might be to camber the smooth cycle track, making it more uncomfortable to walk on than ride on.

In a purpose-built bicycle city, level-yet-cobbled planes could be used in anticipation of walking or very slow cycling, while smooth-yet-cambered planes would anticipate bicycling only. This formula can be applied in various settings. Along linear routes flat cobbled edges to cambered smooth paths would keep pedestrians and cyclists apart without lulling either into a false sense of security or false sense of entitlement.

In the context of cities transitioning to bicycle centricity, one redevelopment zone at a time, and connecting those districts using former industrial waterfronts, rail corridors and similar voids, shared space treatments aren't the main problem. The bigger question is whether riders can somehow be transported to the next district without feeling as though they are racing a time trial. The greatest sources of discomfort would

The 12km stretch of cycleway between the cities of Daejeon and Sejong in South Korea

Covered and back-drafted express routes could shuttle cyclists between new bike friendly enclaves in a city, bypassing districts dominated by cars. Photo of London by Brian Jones. Photo-montage by Harriet Elliot.

Low Line, New York, Raad Studio

surely be rain, heat and headwinds.

Despite what a few apologists for bike transport might say, rain deters a lot of people from cycling to work or to school. Anyone who says commuting by bike ought to be different from driving or taking the bus, by not having a roof, has probably enjoyed way too much praise for riding to work in all weather. These are the proud cyclists, from whose ranks bicycling spokespeople are commonly chosen. A problem comes when they resist design comforts that would get the lily-livered riding as well. As designers we should be more interested in the perspectives of current non-cyclists. More people are likely to start cycling once we put this vulnerable mode on an equal footing with driving or taking the bus, than will be lost if cycling is no longer stoic.

The deterrent of long soaking rides in the rain or sweltering rides in the sun can be solved by the provision of canopies. The 12-km stretch of cycleway between the cities of Daejeon and Sejong in South Korea shows how canopies over bike paths can double as solar panels.

What then of headwinds? If we looked to the future and the best possible marriage of environmental design and bike transport, we would see reasons for dealing with headwinds together, as a collective endeavour. E-bikes are an individualistic response. The problem of wind, though, affects us all equally. Wouldn't it be better to solve the problem with public funds, with windbreaks or backdrafted tubes? Doing so has the added advantage of reducing the need for e-bikes at all. These can be problematic to bike-centric planning. In that scenario e-bikes are a similar kind of menace to cars. Another problem is that e-bikes can accidentally surge forward, making them potentially hazardous to use inside buildings. Two main advantages of a bicycling city over one that uses heavy machines to move people from building to building, are the time savings and conveniences that are possible when we design to let people start riding inside. Unarguably e-bikes are better than cars in urban environments that are designed around cars, but as a central tool about which cities should now be designed they introduce their own irrational set of convolutions.

One group who has looked at backdraft bike tunnels claim the average cyclist could cruise at 40 kph if they and those riding in the same direction all had a roof and walls enclosing their bike route.[41] Despite it being an exaggerated claim, and already disputed,[42] it does make sense that bike highways – if we're going to enclose them so cyclists are protected from the weather like bus riders or drivers – be designed with backdrafting too.

Pictured is a guess as to what a backdrafting structure might look like if it used airspace over a rail line to connect bicycle districts. It shows wind turbines and solar panels on the roof being used to drive fans at both ends of each one-way bike tunnel. The heat and wind that makes cyclists weary become the tailwinds that get them out of there faster.

There is much to be said too for the idea of connecting bicycling districts with tunnels. A group calling for disused subway lines in New York to be made into linear parks have shown how fibre-optic cables can inject underground spaces with enough actual daylight to plant them with trees.[43] In cities with underground shopping arcades it would also be easy to populate underground parks with users other than cyclists.

41
Sustainable Transportation Systems, Inc., 'The Future of Mass Transportation'. Available online: http://www.biketrans.com/index.html, accessed 18 March 2015.

42
John Allen, 'Critique of Bicycle Transportation Systems "Bicycle Tunnel with Tailwinds" Proposal'. Available online: http://www.bikexprt.com/bikepol/facil/biketrans.htm, accessed 18 March 2015.

43
http://www.thelowline.org/.

The special appeal for bike network planners of tunnels is that taking bikes underground means speeding them up upon entry and naturally slowing them down as they leave. They would also give cyclists protection from the elements, especially heat which turns people off of cycling in hotter climates.

We can't leave the topic of backdrafting without considering one implication. Suppose a strong enough backdraft could be produced to double the speed of a box bike, from 15 to 30 kph – right at the threshold of danger but probably not lethal. Would it be possible to think now of doubling the size of a Velotopia model from 15 to 30 km? In the case of New York, vast tracts of poorly-utilized industrial land up to 20 km east of Manhattan might be unlocked for redevelopment without any more strain on existing rail or road networks.

## Other Approaches to Weather Protection

Cars have roofs. Trains and busses have roofs. In past eras walking went under porticos and shop awnings. It was only in the later half of the twentieth-century that the idea took root of leaving some modes – the ones that were vulnerable enough to begin with – exposed to the sun and the rain. Making cycling the main mode of transportation means giving it what principal modes have always enjoyed, and that is weather protection.

London's SkyCycle proposal, first iteration, Sam Martin

Kurilpa Bridge, Brisbane, Cox Rayner Architects

The Shweeb, New Zealand, Geoffrey Barnett

Bear Canyon Bicycle/Pedestrian Bridge, New Mexico, Geoff Adams

The Shweeb, New Zealand, Geoffrey Barnett

# Intermittent Rain Shelters

**While we are in the process of building comprehensive networks of canopies, let us start by building regularly spaced shelters where riders can wait out a short downpour or storm.**

Ubein U Bein Bridge, Mandalay, Burma

Pier 6 Brooklyn, BIG

# Existing and Proposed Bicycle Viaducts

Has there ever been a viaduct built for the car that did not add to the number of cars at street level? Viaducts for cars are one of the major contributors to the numbers of cars seen on the ground plane. The same would be true, surely, of viaducts built for the bike! They would discharge cyclists onto city streets, squeezing out driving. Let us not see bicycling viaducts as attempts to relegate cyclists to lifeless places – even if, in the short term, that is what some proponents are thinking. In the long term they could be like the viaducts that brought so much water to Rome that fountains could flow day and night. Fountains of cyclists spewing from the ends of bicycling viaducts. And may they be as costly as hell! The cost of viaducts built in our cities for cars has never done much to hurt driving.

Copenhagen's Bicycle Snake, DISSING+WEITLING Architecture

SkyCycle proposal for London, second iteration, Foster and Associates

High Bridge Trail, Virginia

Tacoma bicycle bridge, c. 1900

California Cycleway, 1900, Horace Dobbins

High Bridge Trail, Virginia

# Dutch Overpasses

Cyclists see their overpasses and marvel at how much the Dutch seem to spend on bike infrastructure. Let us not forget though that the business case for an overpass usually has more to do with the traffic flowing under than over. In other words, most of these can also be seen as infrastructure for cars. What ought to excite us the most are overpasses that do something for cycling and nothing for driving, like the Nescio Bridge. This bridge linking IJburg to Amsterdam preserves flows of boat traffic using the river, while creating a fast link for cyclists that motorists cannot partake of.

Bicycle overpass in Bruges, Belgium

Nescio Bridge Amsterdam, Wilkinson Eyre Architects

Proposal for bicycle overpass in Givat Shumel, Israel, Nir Ben Natan

Hovenring in Eindhoven, ipv Delft

# Curves and Undulations to Induce Flow States

Time flies when you're having fun. Bike trips feel shorter as well. Optional side attractions that take inspiration from skating, mountain biking or BMX can have zero or negligible impact on trip times but make them feel a lot shorter. They can even improve mental health by putting riders into a flow state. The trick is to keep degrees of difficulty lower than low in situations that scaredy-cat riders cannot avoid. Let's not be so smitten by magical swarms in Amsterdam's Vondelpark or the shared space behind Amsterdam Centraal, for instance, that we foist those levels of excitement onto all riders. Some would prefer peaceful journeys. Let the norm be very low level feelings of swarming and weightlessness, with medium and high level thrills offered as side attractions or detours.

Another advantage of undulating ground planes is they can't be traversed at high speeds using heavy machines with suspension, e.g. cars or motorcycles.

The Simcoe WaveDeck, Toronto, West-8

Vancouver land bridge, Jones & Jones Architecture

Lucky Knot / Dragon King Kong Bridge, Changsha Meixi Lake District, China, by Next Architects

Havøysund Tourist Route, Norway, by Reiulf Ramstad Architects

# Bike Infrastructure that Engages the Senses

The potential tedium of longer stretches of bike path can also be lessened by appeals to the eyes, ears and noses of riders. We're not designing for trucks and cars all moving together at lethal speed. Line markings and warning signs aren't our concerns. Let's design then in the manner of artists for an audience attuned to their senses.

The Twist Bridge, Vlaardingen, West-8

The Van Gogh-Roosegaarde cycle path, Studio Roosegaarde

Proposed Xylophone Bridge in Seoul by Yeon Jae Won and Woo Jeong Heo

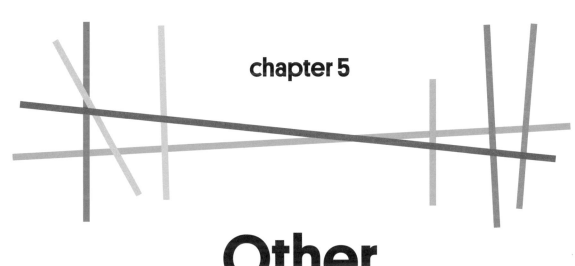

# Other Building Types

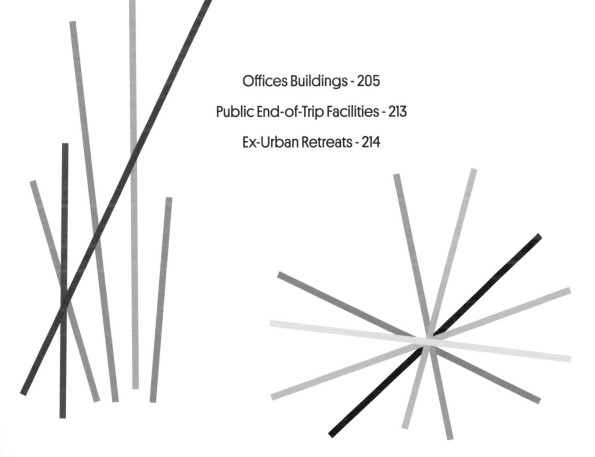

The school's indoor bike parking area was the natural place for the local newspaper to photograph Dr. Anne Lusk and myself on the occasion of the launch of my book Cycle Space.

The far less popular bicycle cage. Photo: Nathan Wheatley

Actual thieves waiting outside the new bike cage. Photo: Anonymous

Indoor cycle track, Amsterdam Google

Cargo Bike reception desk, Amsterdam Google

## Offices Buildings

Is it normal or rare for office workers to eat at their desks? Well it's normal, of course. Whoever worries about spilling a drink on their hard drive or food scraps luring rats and their co-workers catching the plague? Foosball tables are standard features in staff common rooms as well, despite some infinitesimal risk of repetitive strain injuries because none of us have actually had instruction on how to hold foosball handles. If there's an actual danger in the office environment, it is those urns in every staff kitchen, but we don't look sideways at those.

But there is one hazard that is bound to make someone in every office a little bit antsy, and that is bikes on the premises. Bikes parked beside desks. Bikes wheeled into foyers. Even bikes in the bike parking room. They're all a bit suspect. In fact by the way some people glare you would think that bringing a bicycle into a building were written in folklore as the best way to summons Lovecraftian demons, or in actual law as the best way to summons a lawsuit. It is up to every citizen with these kinds of fears, from the cleaner right up to god, to say something if they have seen something. Fighters in this fight cannot rest until all of these two-wheeled contraptions have been relegated to lampposts outside, for vandals or thieves to see to a more permanent fix. Wheelchairs, they're fine. Prams are fine too. But bicycles are a terrorist threat.

One of the best things about cycling being hip with executives now, is that attitudes like those usually do stop with the cleaner. In a bicycle oriented development district, we would hope irrational fears would not even exist. Moreover, we would hope employers and building managers would not only be rational, but outright encouraging of riders parking their bikes how they like.

I am fortunate to have seen how most riders prefer to park their bikes if given all options. In the School of Architecture at the University of Tasmania, where I taught for three years, an unplanned experiment was enacted. The story starts before my arrival, with the school's relocation into a huge, old rail shed in a district with a history of social disadvantage. When students' bikes began to go missing from the bike racks outside, some of the copious ground floor was marked out as an indoor bike park-ing space. When I arrived in 2012 I mistook it as the permanent bike park-ing solution. I soon learned a bike cage was being planned for outside.

In the 18 months before the bike cage arrived I watched the indoor bike parking area filling with more bikes by the day – a classic case of capacity-induced demand stretching capacity. Then came the usual mutterings from a few car-driving colleagues about bikes becoming a menace. People with those complaints always seem blind to the benefits, like a building's reduced carbon footprint if you factor in transport, the health benefits to the students, the potential to rip up some of the park-ing outside and, who knows, build student housing there to save even more people from having to drive, plus the happy vibe resulting from the social interaction going on at the bike racks each day as students from different cohorts struck up conversations about each another's bikes. Suffice to say, not a single bike was stolen or tampered with during these 18 months; the space was, after all, in the middle of a buzzing studio

1
Lloyd Alter, 'Claire Morissette 1950-2007: "Joan of Arc on a Bicycle"', Treehugger (14 August 2007). Available online: http://www.treehugger. com/bikes/claire-moris-sette-1950-2007-joan-of-arc-on-a-bicycle.html, accessed 22 March 2015.

overlooked by two mezzanine levels.

The most informative phase of this (unplanned) experiment came after the bike cage was officially opened (with all of the fanfare), but before the indoor bike area had been removed. Only one student was using the bike cage during this time, and that was the student who had been employed to help make the bike cage. The cheesy graphics about cycling being healthy and green that had been CNC routed on decorative panels screwed to the cage did nothing to make students choose the bike cage over the space they preferred, inside the main building.

For no reason that I can make out except for a fear of Lovecraftian demons the indoor bike racks were removed during the next summer break. The space where the racks used to be promptly filled with a mis-cellaneous collection of old student projects lest anyone park their bike there again. Within weeks of the students returning thieves were back casing the bike cage, waiting for the door to be left ajar. From being an incentive to cycle, bike parking had gone back to being a stressor.

In the 1980s and 1990s, when I was a student, so few of us rode bikes for transport in Australia that we could take our bikes anywhere. I would actually ride my bike into the carpeted hallway of my university library, turn through two right angles within regular sized doorways, and finally ride between my classmates' drawing boards all the way to my workspace on the other side of our studio. There was no rule, or even taboo to prevent me, for the same reason no rule would stop me nude swimming at the North Pole. The first indication of a bike boom, any-where, is the appearance of signs banning bikes, like the ones that so bothered Claire Morissette on Montreal's trains that she started taking ladders on board (there was no rule against ladders!) to demonstrate the absurdity.[1] What she might not have realized is that some of the world's most explicit restrictions on bikes, whether on trains or inside public buildings, are to be found in the Netherlands, the world's leading bike transport nation.

Office building managers and public transport authorities in the Netherlands fear they would be overran if they opened the floodgates on bikes. There are exceptions, like the particular rail services that do allow bikes, or Google's office in Amsterdam that for a short period had a cycle track for a hallway, but these don't typify standard best practice. As a rule, intercity rail passengers are encouraged to leave their bikes in the secure bike parking basements that are being built with every new station upgrade. If they need a bike at the other end of their trip they're encouraged to make use of the OV-fiets bike-sharing scheme.

One thing that would encourage more people in the Netherlands to commute further by bike, would be uncompromisingly wonderful bicycle parking at their destination. Not outside their destination. At their destination. Remember, when the students could choose for themselves between a bike cage, outdoor racks or parking their bikes inside the design studio, they were choosing to leave their bikes inside the design studio. And when bikes were as unproblematic as nude bathing at the North Pole, I was riding all the way to my desk.

Unfortunately, this is not what you see at Utrecht University – one of those rare places where virtually the entire daytime population come

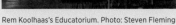

Rem Koolhaas's Educatorium. Photo: Steven Fleming

Herman Hertzberger's Faculty of Science. Photo: Steven Fleming

Shoes outside a temple in Singapore.

Office of Quirky, New York, by Spector Group

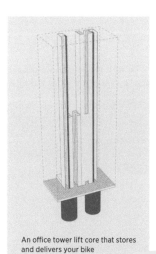

An office tower lift core that stores and delivers your bike

Space filling lower levels of a ramped apartment block, the 8-House by BIG in Copenhagen

Swiss Life's headquarter in Zuric (a.k.a. the "Cocoon") by Camenzing Evolution, 2009.

Hanoi Museum, by GMP Architekten, 2010,        Andalucia's Museum of Memory, in
                                               Granada, Spain, 2009, by Alberto Cam-
                                               po Baeza with double helical ramps.

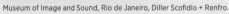
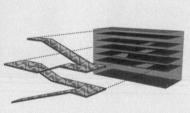

Museum of Image and Sound, Rio de Janeiro, Diller Scofidio + Renfro.

Jaime Jimenez, office building

to the campus by bike and where the building stock represents new Dutch architecture at its very best. Granted, there are many considered bike-parking responses, like the basement bike parking area in Rem Koolhaas's Educatorium and the covered bike-parking field at the entrance to Herman Hertzberger's Faculty of Science.

At each of those buildings cyclists are able to attend to bike chains and pannier bags in a well-lit covered area and walk away from their bikes knowing that judiciously placed windows are helping to ward away thieves. There is still the spectre of theft, though, and the need for bike chains, and the need to take pannier bags off of their bikes, and the slight unease of performing these fiddly tasks in a public space with your back to potential attackers.

The problem of bike parking outside offices or university buildings is a similar problem to shoe storage outside temples in Asia. If Buddhist and Hindu priests didn't believe evil is attached to our shoes, their worshippers would not lose so much time finding their shoes again each time they departed. They would simply keep their shoes on their feet.

The same goes for bikes. We need to jettison any lingering association between bikes and horses from our grandparents' day, and at the same time severe ancestral ties between the modern day office and its pompous progenitors: the Athenaeum Club, the manor house, the palazzo, etcetera. The moment we do, the 'problem' of parked bikes will dissipate into every recess of the workspace and there turn into a plus. Panniers equipped to bikes beside desks could store documents that need to be accessed at work and at home, or at meetings elsewhere. Bikes are also great conversation pieces that help people in office environments build trust, find synergies, feel a sense of belonging, and all of those things corporate coaches say they'll provide for a fee.

Practically, how can we do this? For the naysayers' sake I'll start with the busiest office block type, the tower block, and work backward toward the more manageable types.

Taking a bike in the lift of a residential building, or an office building outside of peak times, is rarely a problem. However, if you have ever tried entering an office tower between 8:30 and 9:00 A.M. you will know there is hardly even room for a briefcase. There is a way, though, for 9-5 workers to have their bikes with them at their workstations.

Depending on how serious we were about incentivizing cycling to work in tall towers, we could give the keen cyclists arriving at rush hour the option of depositing their bikes into automatic storage and retrieval systems (ASRS) and later calling for their bikes to be delivered to their office floor. The diagram shows storage cylinders, like those developed by Giken to store thousands of bikes under stations in Japan, only in this case they are positioned beneath the low and mid-rise lobbies of a central-core office tower.[2] Those entering the building who might like their bikes with them later would pass the security checkpoint like anyone else and deposit their bike for temporary holding in the underground storage cylinder. After riding the passenger lift to their floor like anyone else, they could call for their bike to be delivered by ASRS equipment fitted within the vertical shaft (coloured blue in the diagram). On its own this is not

2
http://www.giken.com/
en/developments/
eco_cycle/.

a flawless solution, but in conjunction with a suite of other bike parking options – like a ramp-access basement with secure entry – it would be a pièce de résistance in a bike-friendly tower.

The example above is mainly to show that vertical circulation for bikes can't be dismissed as too hard. It is more likely that tall office towers would rarely be called for in a bicycle city. They exist in places like midtown Manhattan because thousands of businesses all want to be within walking distance of Grand Central Station. But as discussed in an earlier chapter, CBDs in bicycling cities are likely to be as much as 25-times larger in area than CBDs designed around walking, for the simple reason that bikes shrink linear distance by a factor of five. That means a bicycle oriented city's demand for office space could largely be met by space available on the ground floor of apartment blocks.

The only exception might be mid-rise buildings for single tenants. As the example of Swiss Life's headquarter in Zuric (a.k.a. the 'Cocoon') by Camenzing Evolution illustrates, a spiral parti is one way to design an office building that, if management were to allow it, would welcome riders wanting to keep their bikes at their desks.

Countless more buildings show that courtyards, or atria, of sufficient diameter can incorporate spiralling ramps.

Alternatively ramped access can be added to facades. While architects need to be mindful of the impact upon workers' outlooks if ramps cross in front of their windows, one advantage of exterior ramps is they can mitigate heat load especially on the west side of an office building. (Note that in the case of secure office buildings, ramps should only be accessible from the secure zone in the lobby, and not from the outside.) While it may be too steep to ride down, Diller Scofidio + Renfro's 'vertical promenade' on the face of their Museum of Image and Sound in Rio de Janeiro offers an elegant example of an elevation that integrates ramps.

The following student project by Jaime Jimenez uses ramps as brise-soleil on the western façade of a bike-access office. The ramp kills two birds at once, cooling a building type that generates heat from bodies and equipment such as computers, while at the same time letting every staff member bring their bike to their desk and leave more quickly at the end of the day than co-workers in crowded lifts. This student has cleverly raised the secure lift foyer from the ground by one story using a ramp. This has allowed him to use the roof of a retail podium as an outdoor bike parking area for those who aren't as precious about their bikes – who perhaps don't have so far to ride that they need a great bike. Bike parking on the podium roof is overlooked by all of the offices yet not in view of passers-by, making it more secure than street level, or even basement bike parking.

Not surprisingly, some of the most inspiring experiments in building typology that can inform architecture for bikes have been designed to bring cars into buildings. UN Studio's Mercedes Benz Museum will make a fine office building for cyclists if cars become a thing of the past.

Car companies do not have a total monopoly, though. In designing the Taipei head office of bike brand Giant, Studiobase Architects and Reborn Studio have included a curved bike ramp winding its way from

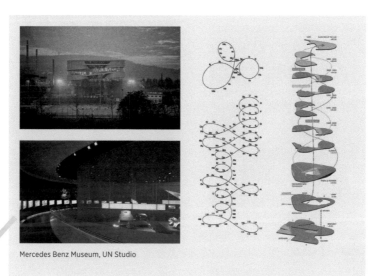

Mercedes Benz Museum, UN Studio

Giant Headquarter Building, Taipei, Studiobase Architects + Reborn Studio

An appropriate use of a bicycle as a piece of a wall art.

Bike hoists seem to give bikes pride of place, like pieces of art, but are a hindrance for regular cyclists. Left: IDEO San Francisco Offices, Jensen Architects. Right: GAE house, Atelier Bow-Wow, Tokyo.

# chapter 5  Other Building Types

Bicycle Tree, The Bigloo and the Bicycle Hanger

De blob in Eindhoven, Wytze Patijn's Fietsappel at Alphen aan den Rijn station and the Gulskogen Bicycle Hotel in Drammen, Norway by MMW Architects

the street to an exhibition space one level up. The geometry of the ramp sets up an irregular pattern that then informs the design of the façade.

To end this section on bike parking in offices, a reminder that most bikes are not wall art. Some are, but not the ones we ride to work, or use to run errands a few times a day, or even ride to the photocopy room in an office designed for riding inside. Those bikes should not have to be mounted each time they're dismounted.

The earlier analogy with hand basins should drive home this point. If washing our hands after the toilet required some tricky manoeuvres to lower the basin down from the roof, fewer people would be washing their hands after the toilet and more of us would be dying from infectious diseases. Adding to the time it takes to hop on a bike is a similar deterrent to leaving the office by bike. Not only do frequent fast trips increase peoples' health, they add to opportunities for face to face interaction with a wider range of potential suppliers, collaborators and clients.

## Public End-of-Trip Facilities

A city stocked with buildings that allowed people to use their bikes within shops, their homes and their places of work would obviously reduce the percentage of cyclists who would require secure bicycle parking. Most would keep their bikes with them wherever they went. However, there is still a range of destination types that draw many people at once, and bring them into very tight quarters, and would therefore need to be served by secure bike parking stations. These include train stations, sports stadiums, nightclubs and theatres. If a city existed where 90 per cent of trips were by bike, bicycle parking structures around these kinds of venues would need to be quite enormous.

The resurgence in popularity in urban cycling has seen many designers patenting, prototyping or quite often just drawing, automatic storage and retrieval systems (ASRS) that could be small and dispersed throughout cities. The examples shown here are the Bicycle Tree,[3] The Bigloo[4] and the Bicycle Hanger.[5]

Notwithstanding the apparent reliability of the Eco-Cycle ASRS devices in Japan (though, their failure on the evening of Japan's earthquake in 2011 did leave thousands of people with a long walk back home), one must be especially suspicious of small and specialized machines like these breaking down. As the Dutch have found with their municipal-secure bike parking stations that they build in conjunction with their train stations, there is really no substitute for a station large enough to warrant a paid parking attendant issuing and collecting tickets that owners produce when retrieving their bike. No system has been found that is faster or more reliable than a bike parking station where people deposit and retrieve their bikes simply by riding them to a rack, and where security is handled at one entry point by an attendant scanning tags. The only drawback is parking stations like these have to be large. That means siting them within walking distance of multiple crowd-drawing venues.

It doesn't hurt either to make them architecturally prominent like

3
http://www.treehugger.
com/cars/bike-tree-
locked-bicycle-storage.
html.

4
http://www.bigloo.es/.

5
http://www.design-
buzz.com/10-highly-
innovative-bike-stands-
urban-areas/.

6
http://www.designboom.
com/architecture/massi-
miliano-fuksas-de-blob-
at-september-18-square/.

7
http://www.architectuur.
nl/project/fietsappel-
alphen-aan-den-rijn/.

8
http://inhabitat.com/
gulskogen-bicycle-
hotel-stashes-over-a-
hundred-bikes-behind-an-
intricate-filigree-facade
/#ixzz3AvtjJVaD&i.

9
Committee on Aero-
nautics Research and
Technology for Environ-
mental Compatibility, For
Greener Skies: Reducing
Environmental Impacts
of Aviation, (Washington:
National Academies Press,
2002).

10
John M. Polimen, The
Jevons Paradox and the
Myth of Resource Efficiency
Improvements (London:
Earthscan, 2012).

11
Janet E. Dickinson, Les
Lumsdo, Slow Travel and
Tourism (London: Earth-
scan, 2010).

12
For example, see the
2013 Houses (Australia)
Awards, available online:
http://housesawards.com.
au; and also examples of
other architectural media
extolling the virtues of
architecture in hinterland
or beach locations: http://
architectureau.com/arti-
cles/hill-plains-house/;
http://architectureau.
com/articles/wolgan-
valley-resort-and-spa/; or
http://inhabitat.com/7-
gorgeous-eco-resorts-for-
a-green-escape/.

13
U.S. Green Building
Council LEED, 'LEED Case
Study #69 The Chesa-
peake Bay Foundation's
Philip Merrill Environmental Center' (CBF Merrill
Environmental Center,
2008). Available online:
http://leedcasestudies.
usgbc.org/overview.
cfm?ProjectID=69, ac-
cessed 20 March 2014.

14
In a detailed study exam-
ining the levels of energy
use associated with transport in variously located
workplaces, Naess and
Sandberg (1996) found
that ' . . . data indicate

the following examples: the entrance to Massimiliano Fuksas's de blob in Eindhoven;[6] Wytze Patijn's Fietsappel at Alphen aan den Rijn station;[7] and the Gulskogen Bicycle Hotel in Drammen, Norway by MMW Architects.[8]

## Ex-Urban Retreats

In setting the stage for this book, we considered the need for a sustainable model of urban development that the world's richest 2 billion would choose out of self-interest and in so doing inspire 5 billion more with an alternative to car-centric cities. Well it is hard to imagine any model of city living achieving such popularity if it does not allow residents to occasionally escape their daily concerns. The question is this: can the whole world's population enjoy getaways to the coast or the country in a sustainable way?

Some would argue that neither plane or car travel pose a threat to the planet, that engines and refined fuels are becoming so efficient that one day flying and driving on highways will be essentially green.[9] They are ignoring Jevons's paradox, the phenomenon whereby efficiencies designed to conserve resources lead to more uses for those resources and eventually net increases in their consumption.[10] Jevons saw that efficient coal burners led to wider uses for coal and the need for even more coalmines. In our times it is possible to see how doubling the fuel efficiencies of the automotive and aviation industries would only quadruple their overall scale.

Rather than asking scientists how we can sustainably do what we want to do now, we could be asking the artists (film-makers, novelists, architects, etcetera) for something different to want. As for architects, not only do we have the rational design skills to double the efficiencies of buildings and cities, but we can double the attractiveness of sustainable living, including sustainable tourism. The discussion should be less about eco-tourism (which can mean flying or driving to a resort that has composting loos) and more about what some are now calling 'slow tourism', a philosophy of travel that puts emphasis on the journey itself, starting from the home, and that favours sustainable modes such as trains.[11]

Working in our favour, if we want to promote slow tourism over flying and car-driving holidays, is the sense one can have that both flying and driving are nouveau riche novelties. They have symbolic importance to first the generations who get access to each, but are seen for what they are by generations to follow. Parents of teenaged children will have seen this, how proud announcements at dinner that the whole family will be going on a plane can be met with indifference. If you have ever felt that deflation think back to your own reactions when you were that age and your own parents announced a car-driving holiday; many of our generation would have sooner been sent to stay with our aunties. For the parents, offering a child an opportunity to cross the country in a car in the 1980s, or the world in a plane in the 2000s, is a sacrificial love offering, tantamount to giving them a private school education. To the child who has done it before, and whose unaffected memory is of being cooped up for ages then dragged around to museums, a long trip in a car or a plane is not a reward. It's some kind of torture. Thinking this way is cause for hope that slow tourism might outshine flying and driving, one day, when the whole world is wealthy and bored by both options.

More discouraging are attitudes among the architectural profession. There is a natural reluctance to accept, as a category of environment impacts related to buildings, all of those impacts rolling out of the car parks that are as much a part of architects' projects as the features to reduce heating and cooling. Where architects ought to be shaming each other for accepting commissions that generate avoidable car trips, or at the very least educating their clients, they are giving each other awards for green window dressing. Scroll through any list of industry awards nominations for sustainable architecture and you will mostly find magnets for car trips. If you want to depress yourself even more, look at what sells advertising space in online and glossy house magazines: cabin porn.[12] You find it accompanied by words on the architect's magical powers of climate control using oddly cranked plan forms – no mention of how one might get to a mountaintop without burning oil.

In 2002, the Philip Merrill Environmental Centre became the first ever building to receive a Platinum rating from LEED for its energy efficiency.[13] In addition to daily energy use, the designers, Smith Group Inc., considered the smallest details of the building's environmental impacts, from how it would be demolished, to the 'light pollution' it would emit after dark. What they failed to account for was the building's transport energy intensity that would have been lower if the Philip Merrill Environmental Centre was located in downtown Annapolis.[14] The clients left premises to which many of their staff could walk or cycle, or take a bus, to occupy a new building 16 km out of town. A slow cyclist would lose more than two hours a day to commuting if they had to work there.

Environmental ratings tools like LEED in the US, BREEAM in Europe or Green Star in Australia, do not adequately penalize buildings that, due to their exurban locations, encourage most users to travel by car. They focus on the ecological footprints of the buildings themselves while downplaying all the negative externalities associated with car dependency. These go beyond oil consumption and emissions, to include loss of flora and habitats and turning native fauna into roadkill due to road building and widening,[15] the human death toll from road accidents,[16] the cost of medically treating a sedentary population,[17] noise pollution from cars, contamination of water catchment areas with pollutants from cars[18] and the energy embodied in each car as a result of its manufacture and shipping.[19]

Since the Velotopia model has been couched in terms of the world's total emissions, there can be little countenancing (at least not in this book) of construction outside city limits, that is to say outside the 15-km-wide circle of interest in which those pursuing the Velotopian dream agree to all live, work, shop and send our children to school. That leaves us only with the (non-)problem of buildings for non-urban work like farming and mining (that have to exist, so may as well be accessed by cars), and the real problem of how to build places of respite from the city.

This can mean cabins on hiking trails, tourist facilities reachable only by sailboat or rail, complexes at the end of cable car routes or, as

that a central location of workplaces within the urban area seems to be favourable if the aim is to reduce energy use and private car commuting. However . . . transport energy impacts of workplace locations depend not only on the commuting trips of employees, but also on freight transport, trips for the firm, and the journeys made by visitors.' All these factor would be key components impacting the transport energy intensity of the Phillip Merrill Centre.

15
P. Daigle, 'A Summary of the Environmental Impacts of Roads, Management Responses, and Research Gaps: A Literature Review', *Journal of Ecosystems and Management*, Vol. 10 (2010) No. 3, 65-89.

16
R. Tooth, 'The Cost of Road Crashes: A Review of Key Issues', Southbank, VIC: Australasian Railway Association (2010). Available online: http://www.ara.net.au/UserFiles/file/Publications/TheCostof-RoadCrashesReport.pdf

17
F. W. Booth and M.V. Chakravarthy, 'Cost and Consequences of Sedentary Living: New Battleground for an Old Enemy', *President's Council on Physical Fitness Research Digest*, Vol. 3 (2002) No. 16, 1-8; I. Janssen, 'Health Care Costs of Physical Inactivity in Canadian Adults', *Applied Physiology, Nutrition and Metabolism*, No. 37 (2012), 803-806; R. J. Shephard, 'Is Active Commuting the Answer to Population Health?', *Sports Medicine*, Vol. 38(2008) No. 9, 751-758.

18
R. T. T. Forman, 'Estimate of the Area Affected Ecologically by the Road System in the United States', *Conservation Biology*, Vol. 14 (2000) No. 1, 31-35; S.C. Trombulak and C.A. Frissell, 'Review of Ecological Effects of Roads on Terrestrial and Aquatic Communities', *Conservation Biology*, Vol. 14 (2000) No. 1, 18-30.

19
Treloar, G. J., Love, P. E. D., & Crawford, R. H. (2004). Hybrid Life-Cycle Inventory for Road Construction and Use. Journal of Construction Engineering and Management, 130(1), 43-49.

20
Rodrigo Cáceres Céspedes, 'Endless Cycling', *Arch Daily* (17 February 2014). Available online: http://www.archdaily.com/477224/endless-cycling-rodrigo-caceres-cespedes/, accessed 4 February 2015.

21
http://www.onomichi-u2.com/en/hotel_cycle.html. 22 'Built for Bicycles', available online: http://www.belleislehome.com/2010/08/built-for-bicycles.html.

23
Jacques Derrida, *Of Grammatology* (Baltimore: The Johns Hopkins University Press, 1997).

24
Gerd-Helge Vogel, 'Mobility: The Fourth Dimension in the Fine Arts and Architecture', *Contemporary Aesthetics*, Special Vol. (2005) No. 1.

25
Robert W. Marks, *The Dymaxion World of Buckminster Fuller* (New York: Anchor Press, 1960).

interests us here, places to stay along bicycling trails. Some notable precedents are Rodrigo Cáceres Céspedes's Endless Cycling pavilion with a triangulated structure that evokes a bike frame;[20] Hotel Cycle in Hiroshima by Suppose Design Office with wheel channels flanking the stairs, hooks on suite walls for guests to hang bikes and an entry designed to let cyclists check in while still on their bikes;[21] and the most intriguing example, due to its size and its age, the bicycle pavilion on Belle Isle Park, Detroit from 1898 by the architect Edward A. Schilling. Now an athletics pavilion, it reminds us that in the late 1800s cycling in America was an even more popular way of escaping the city than taking a train.

The first of these three examples has a bike-like aesthetic. The second has features that would seem puzzling until you realized they were for bikes. The third has a balcony that reminds at least one regular visitor of a bicycle wheel.[22] While none of that is remarkable what it does point to is the specialness of arriving by bike. Cycling has never been such a mundane way of reaching a destination some distance from town that an architect would pass on the opportunity to represent this mode of transport in a structure built for it.

Ways architects might represent modes of transportation in buildings is something I discussed in my last book, *Cycle Space* (2012), in that case by referring to Jacques Derrida's notion of an absent presence.[23] I argued that since motion is present by its conspicuous absence from buildings, it is the first thing architects try to represent when designing a building they know cannot move. Earlier in this book I cited Gerd-Helge Vogel who argues that mobility is a fourth dimension, of sorts, within architecture.[24]

The most useful thing that can be done here, in making that point that architecture can inspire people to make their escapes from the city by bike rather than unsustainable modes, is to remind readers of the instigator role architecture played in the first half of the twentieth century, for it was architecture as much as any other mode of communication that implanted the idea in the cultural imagination that driving should be the natural way to leave town. Until then, as we see by the scale of the Bicycle Pavilion, cycling had been a more popular means, especially in the United States. A century later, unsustainable modes have a virtual monopoly, with aeroplanes being the first choice for travel from city to city, and cars being so popular out in the country that cycling there is often too frightening for most to consider.

One thing architects did to bring this about was give us the house of the future. As if to rebuke the very notion of not owning a car, the house of the future in the late 1920s was always located outside city limits, with the most potent versions lifted off of the ground so that cars could park under. The greatest provocateur of the time was Buckminster Fuller who took the extra step of designing his very own car and showing where it and the owner's own plane would go under their house.[25]

Another lesson of the time is to lead by blind faith. No one could have been certain in the 1920s that mass car ownership would ever eventuate, much less have an impact on urban planning. In 1925 when Walter Gropius was designing the Bauhaus School in Dessau, Germany's *autobahn* network was still just a pipe dream for a handful of absolute

Philip Merrill Environmental Centre was located in downtown Annapolis

The bicycle pavilion on Belle Isle Park, Detroit from 1898 by the architect Edward A. Schilling

Rodrigo Cáceres Céspedes's Endless Cycling pavilion

Hotel Cycle in Hiroshima by Suppose Design Office

Buckminster Fuller

Bauhaus School in Dessau

row 1:  SANAA, 3Gatti Architecture Studio, Luka Vlahovic
row 2: Friedensreich Hundertwasser, Peter Eisenmann, Claudiu Ionescu
row 3: Foreign Office Architects, Toyo Ito, BIG, Architects NL
row 4: Zaha Hadid Architects, BIG, BIG, Kuan Wang
row 5: Steven Holl, BIG, BIG
row 6: JDS Architects, HOK Sport, Architects NL

optimists. It would be another 12 years before Hitler would make highway building an official priority along with a car for the people, the Volkswagen. This was all years off, yet if we study Gropius's design and all the preliminary plans (the ones pictured here by Carl Fieger, not Gropius himself), we see a bold split in each iteration right where a roadway was envisioned passing under the building.

With as much conviction as any church architect who believes Christ's second coming will be from the direction they have pointed their nave, Gropius designed the Bauhaus School as a welcoming embrace for students and teachers to come to his building by car. The symphony of architecture and moving traffic that Gropius has created might as well have been led by a one armed conductor: the roadway, now Bauhausplatz, still hadn't been built when Gropius left for the U.S., and even today is more of a laneway than the motorway hinted at by the design.

One of the ways early modernism changed the way we all live (or how the Bauhaus changed our house)[26] was by saying a main entrance for cars, and an overall house composition inflected to encompass an integrated garage, was the modern way of designing. As early as 1941, just over a decade after the first works of carchitecture,[27] and 20 years before car ownership had trickled down to the masses, Sigfried Giedion was proclaiming an entirely new zeitgeist defined by the handful of highways and drive-in houses that had so far come into existence.[28] There are many factors we can point to as having led to the rise of the car (its utility, its champions like Henry Ford, all of the oil fields in Texas, etcetera), but high among them is the catalytic power of visionary architecture. It showed people that cars were not just beautiful objects in their own right (although architects did much in their spare time to promote them as such)[29] but they could also be keys for unlocking a new style of living in a freestanding house amidst greenery.

What architecture can show people today is the possibility of a retreat from the city that begins the moment they leave their apartment. Instead of fighting city traffic until breaking out onto the highway, we could be cycling from our apartments onto networks of greenways built along urban waterways and former rail easements. Architects can help people imagine bike touring holidays on the safe touring-trail networks that most nations are already in the process of building.

That still leaves one question. What can be done, architecturally, whether through style or special rewards for bike travellers, to mark something like a resort or pavilion as a special place to head to by bike, rather than in a car? The best way to answer, without turning this into a book about my own stylistic proclivities, is to answer with pictures. The following photo gallery highlights projects that are inviting of cycling in some way or another, starting with a number of projects with undulating floors and/or trafficable roofs that any among us who still likes to play would be very tempted to ride on.

26
Tom Wolfe, *From Bauhaus to Our House* (London: Picador, 1981).

27
Jonathan Bell, *Carchitecture: When the Car and the City Collide* (Basel: Birkhäuser, 2001).

28
Sigfried Giedion, *Space, Time and Architecture: The Growth of a New Tradition* (Cambriage, MA: Harvard University Press, 1941).

29
See: Ivan Margolius, *Automobiles by Architects* (Hoboken: John Wiley and Sons, 2000). See also: Antonio Amado, *Voiture Minimum: Le Corbusier and the Automobile* (Cambridge, MA: The MIT Press, 2011).

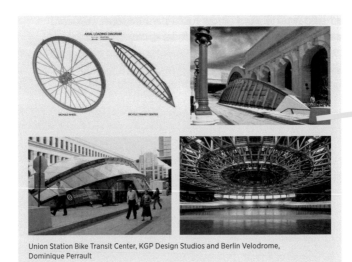

Union Station Bike Transit Center, KGP Design Studios and Berlin Velodrome,
Dominique Perrault

"Cycle" by Richard Serra

Aula Medica, Wingårdh Arkitektkontor

NE Apartments, Tokyo, Yuji Nakae, Akiyoshi Takagi
and Hirofumi Ohno

Bilbao Guggenheim Museum, Frank Gehry

When architecture was being used to promote the car in the 1920s and 1930s, it was common to make buildings that were like cars. Witness the metal panelling crowning the Chrysler Building in New York. Shown here are two projects for bikes that refer to the compression ring structure of a bicycle wheel.

With buildings that are to be ridden to, via or through a unique opportunity exists to address a viewer who is not perpendicular to the horizon and whose view of the world becomes a blur when descending, then very detailed as they reach a crest and lose speed. In a rare paper to ask if there is anything distinctive about cyclists' view of the city that urban designers should take account of Ann Forsyth and Kevin Krizek note that their heights, positions and speeds are different from that of pedestrians.[30] To those three we might add leaning, which intensifies with speed and acuteness of corners, and thus might be responded to with buildings like the ones shown here.

30
Ann Forsyth and Kevin Krizek, 'Urban Design: Is There a Distinctive View from the Bicycle?', *Journal of Urban Design*, Vol. 16 (2011) No. 4, 531-549.

ДАТА / ВРЕМЯ

**7.10**

СЕГОДНЯ ВЕЛОСИПЕДИСТОВ

**168**

ВСЕГО ВЕЛОСИПЕДИСТОВ

**31638**

#ЛюбимыйАльметьевск
ГОРОД ДЛЯ ЖИЗНИ,
РАБОТЫ И ОТДЫХА!

SmarTrack.

# chapter 6

# We Have Decluttered Our Homes, Now Let's Declutter Our Cities

## In Relation to the History of Urban Design

Anyone who has not heard Enrique Peñalosa, Janette Sadik-Khan or Mikael Colville-Andersen speak might not realize just how enthralling their success stories about urban cycling and urban renewal can be. Most of us live in cities where bike plans are gathering dust. Their cities' bike plans have been put into action. Now we all want to hear, live and in person, their blow-by-blow tales. For speakers like these on the urbanist talk circuit, having success stories is like having hit songs if you are a singer.

There is a huge difference, though, between what New York and Copenhagen have brought into being (principally, a third layer in their road matrix) and what this book is proposing: a new development mindset. Without wishing to diminish achievements it would be great to see replicated all over the world, the proliferation of cycle tracks has more in common with the proliferation of roundabouts in the late 1980s, or the widening of carriageways back in the 1960s, than a new development model with new types of buildings and public realm treatments.

What this book is proposing is a proliferation of car-free redevelopment districts interconnected by greenways along former bulk-haulage routes in the first world. That is not an end itself, but rather a response to global warming and population control in the developing world. The ultimate goal is that Velotopian layers in first-world cities serve as beacons to the developing world. What they need from us, and what we need to give them, is a vision of a faster and more prosperous city that is non-polluting. The car-and-sprawl model we are presenting them now is a kind of suicide pact.

An idea so vast yet fuzzy as Velotopia is not like Copenhagen's plan for more pedestrian bridges or New York's plan to forge on with more cycle tracks. It is more like the image of the Futurama from 1939 or the Garden Cities model from 1898.

The Futurama and Garden City visions weren't exactly enactable blueprints. For the purposes of the following discussion, it would be better to think of them as town planning manifestations of peoples' lusts at the time. Try to imagine the lust city dwellers must have been feeling by the late 1800s for lives amidst greenery after having all rushed to cities for jobs. Ebenezer Howard's Garden Cities vision satiated that lust. Or imagine the lust factory workers must have had by the late 1930s for machines of their own, given their experience with machines in their factory jobs and all the times they would have seen their bosses using private cars for transport. That is the lust Norman Bel Geddes was feeding with his Futurama pavilion. We can imagine Velotopia as something that might satiate our lust, a lust we see echoed in the culture more generally, for a lighter weight life without those machines.

Seeing how the aim here is to satiate a kind of a lust, it is important that past success stories be identified that speak to such a lofty and nebulous enterprise. After all, we are not just talking about a 'bike plan' or 'consultant's report'. We are contributing to something historians might one day look back on and refer to as a 'cultural turn' or 'paradigm shift'.

Before looking at some case studies from history (quite distant history, in one case) let's be reminded that the flames being stoked are already established, especially in contemporary architecture. As was pointed out at the start of this book, the vast majority of small to medium scale projects in *The Phaidon Atlas of 21st Century World Architecture* are low-tech in their aesthetic. Rough-hewn timber and rusticated masonry have taken over from white walls that look as though they rolled from a machine, while not since 1980s British hi tech has it been fashionable to festoon the exterior of buildings with apparatus.

Underlying this is the 'critical arriere-garde' disposition toward new technology that Kenneth Frampton identified and that is now completely normative within architectural practice. We know it is normative by the way Rem Koolhaas was able to position himself as a reactionary with his exhibition at the Venice Biennale in 2014 that asked architects to reconnect with technology. A lot of us don't care in the slightest.

So the cultural turn is already a fact. The shift can be tracked back as far as the lunar landing, which hardly got anybody as excited as NASA was hoping. All we are asking is that city planners and designers of large public buildings give society at large what the gentry have been demanding in their own homes: a tighter ration of machines so their lives might be leaner, more efficient and connected to the sensorial world.

## The Body, the Primitive Hut, the Machine and the Traditional City

Here now are four case studies examining the successful implementation of whole new ways of seeing architecture and urban design. Each success story features a societal longing, or lust, and a strategy that architects used to convince patrons that their buildings would somehow help satiate that longing or lust. The first, as mentioned, is virtually ancient.

Liane Lefaivre's book about the 1499 architectural treatise and novel *Hypnerotomachia Poliphili*[1] (which she argues was written by Leon Battista Alberti) vividly describes the air of permissiveness that arose during the Renaissance and that led to Bonfire of the Vanities. A reaction was brewing against the old Augustinian/medieval view that the body and spirit were separate and that the body was cursed. To some extent attitudes had been changing ever since the 'Renaissance of the twelfth century', a term used to describe the period in which St Thomas Aquinas synthesized Christian doctrine with Aristotle's view that the sensorial world was a source of true knowledge.[2] The year 1499, though, marks an apogee. The body stops being seen as an illusionary trap for the soul and instead becomes an object of lust as well as a paragon of beauty for architects to aspire to. If you don't know the story, the main character of *Hypnerotomachia Poliphili* has a dream within a dream where the women and buildings are all so desirous he has penetrative sex, not with women, but with buildings, on three separate occasions – or at least that's the number of times that Lefaivre can find.

All this could be dismissed as trivial smut if the *Hypnerotomachia Poliphili* were printed in a manner equivalent to an X-rated novel today. However, in its typesetting and illustrations it actually had the highest

1
Liane Lefaivre, *Leon Battista Alberti's Hypnerotomachia Poliphili: Re-Cognizing the Architectural Body in the Early Italian Renaissance* (Cambridge, MA: The MIT Press, 1997).

2
Charles Homer, *The Renaissance of the Twelfth Century* (Cambridge, MA: Harvard University Press, 1927).

3
Johann Joachim Winckel-
mann, *Reflections on the
painting and sculpture of
the Greeks: With Instruc-
tions for the Connoisseur,
and an Essay on Grace in
Works of Art* (London:
1965), originally published
in German in 1755.
Available online: https://
archive.org/details/reflec-
tionsonpai00winc.

4
Edmund Burke, *A Philo-
sophical Inquiry into the
Origin of Our Ideas of The
Sublime and Beautiful
With Several Other Addi-
tions* (London: Thomas
M'lean, Haymarket, 1757).
Available online: http://
www.bartleby.com/24/2/,
accessed 13 March 2015.

5
William Gilpin, *Observa-
tions on the River Wye:
Observations on the River
Wye, and Several Parts of
South Wales, &c. Relative
Chiefly to Picturesque
Beauty; Made in the
Summer of the Year 1770*
(London: 1782). Available
online: https://archive.
org/details/observation-
sonr00gilpgoog, accessed
13 March 2015.

6
Eugène Emmanuel
Viollet-le-Duc, *Entretiens
sur l'architecture* (Paris:
Q. Morel et cie, 1863).
Available online: https://
archive.org/details/
entretienssurla00goog
accessed 13 March 2015.

7
Filippo Tommaso Marinet-
ti, 'Futurist Manifesto', in:
R.W. Flint (Ed.) *Marinetti:
Selected Writings* (New
York: Farrar, Straus and
Giroux, 1972), 39-44. First
published in *Le Figaro*
(20 February 1909).

8
Antonio Sant'Elia
'Messaggio', *Nuove
Tendenze* (1914).

9
Le Corbusier, *Vers une
architecture* (Paris: Les
éditions G. Crès, 1923).

production values of any book since the advent of printing, a fact that undoubtedly helped it inspire another two centuries of architecture that was analogous to the body. Thus we see Alberti's writings on architecture and art often referring back to the body as the perfect adumbration of the celestial order, Francesco di Giorgio Martini giving us all of his memorable drawings showing how the proportions of buildings and building elements can be derived from the body; Gianlorenzo Bernini and Francesco Borromini designing church fronts with welcoming arms and chests swelled with air; and let's not forget the emblem of the Renaissance, Leonardo da Vinci's depiction of the body's proportions as originally described by Vitruvius.

The next comparable interval in the history of architecture was marked by a new paragon, this time the mythical idea of the primitive hut as put forward in Marc-Antoine Laugier's *Essai sur l'architecture* (1753). Drawing attention to a lesser known passage in Vitruvius (not the one about the body's proportions that fascinated Leonardo and company, but one about Greek temples being petrified versions of wooden huts), Laugier gave architects just the right paragon considering their two main proclivities in the eighteenth century. Proclivity one: a lust for travel to see ancient Greek temples such as the Parthenon, something that comes through in Johann Winckelmann's *Reflections on the Painting and Sculpture of the Greeks* (1765).[3] Proclivity two: an even more pronounced lust for science and reason than was present during the Italian Renaissance. Laugier was writing in the age of the Enlightenment, that is, in the aftermath of Galileo, Descartes and Newton.

Some important ideas would come along in the eighteenth and nineteenth centuries like the sublime,[4] the picturesque[5] and structural rationalism,[6] but none so big that art and architectural historians have used them as labels for 'ages'. We have seen how there was an age of humanism and how it had its own paragon, the body, then how there was the age of the Enlightenment with the primitive hut as its paragon. There would not be another agreed upon 'age' until a new paragon arrived to replace the previous two, and that would not happen until there was a new societal lust that neither the primitive hut or the body were suited to quell.

This time the lust would be for speed, of two types: first, the speed of a 'racing car with its bonnet adorned with giant tubes' that Filippo Marinetti described in his manifesto of Futurism;[7] and second, the speed of change that Antonio Sant'Elia wrote about in his manifesto of Futurist architecture where he refers to a 'bustling shipyard, every part agile, mobile and dynamic', because, as Sant'Elia argues, 'the futurist house must [likewise] become a kind of gigantic machine'.[8] The age in question is the machine age. Its paragons are machines, generally, but especially machines of transportation, like aeroplanes and airships. Nine times out of ten, though, the actual machine they referred to was the automobile. Le Corbusier left no doubt about the car's adumbration of the Greek temple/primitive hut as the paragon for the new age with the layout of this page in *Vers une architecture*.[9]

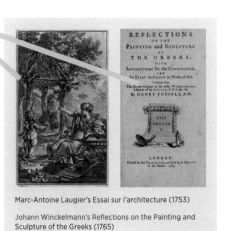

Marc-Antoine Laugier's Essai sur l'architecture (1753)

Johann Winckelmann's Reflections on the Painting and Sculpture of the Greeks (1765)

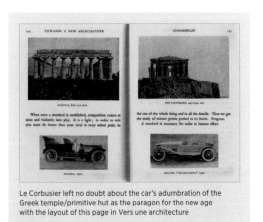

Le Corbusier left no doubt about the car's adumbration of the Greek temple/primitive hut as the paragon for the new age with the layout of this page in Vers une architecture

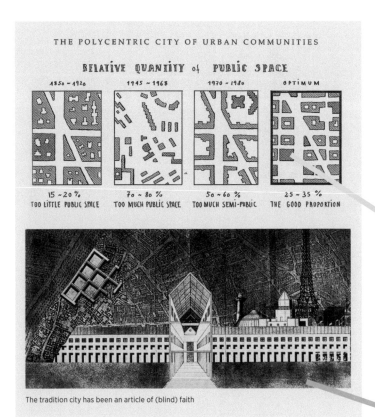

THE POLYCENTRIC CITY OF URBAN COMMUNITIES

The tradition city has been an article of (blind) faith

They wouldn't know Aldo from Valentino

Yakov Chernikhov's simple device

Three ages: the age of humanism, the Enlightenment and the machine age. Three paragons: the body, the primitive hut and the car. But that is not where this story ends – not quite. Even though car land is still proliferating at the edges of our cities today, producing mega malls, freeways and drive-in fast food joints, intellectuals have been advocating an alternative model of urban development (with yet another paragon) ever since it first became apparent that the machine age was eroding communities and our economic autonomy as individuals.

From the mid-1950s the situationists in Paris,[10] led by Guy Debord, were advocating what Debord termed 'the derive' – basically getting drunk and walking across the city to prove to yourself that the road and rail networks don't govern your life.[11] Influenced by Marxist doctrines, they believed machines of transportation in a capitalist democracy were rigged to take people to work in the morning, to the shops in the evening to spend all they had earned, then home to rest so they could go again the next day. Walking became an act of resistance, as it remains for modern day psychogeographers, who continue the tradition started in Paris.[12]

The mid-1950s is also when Josep Lluís Sert initiated the world's first 'urban design' degree program at the Harvard Graduate School of Design. Like Debord, Sert was focused on the experience of the pedestrian. He was also acutely critical of what he described as 'the uncontrolled sprawl of our communities' fearing life behind the wheel of a car was depriving people of the chance interaction that once made communities strong.[13] What we see in the 1950s is a hankering for a less capitalistic and more convivial life. More walking was seen as the answer.

Sert's new GSD degree program and related symposia provided a platform for a generation of urban design theorists focused on the pedestrian experience. In the 1960s, they included Kevin Lynch,[14] Gordon Cullen[15] and, the most famous, Jane Jacobs.[16] By the 1970s the people promoting pedestrian-centric theories of urban design were the ones mentioned earlier as having led Anthony Vidler to announce a new paragon.[17] According to Vidler, the main players were Rob and Léon Krier and Aldo Rossi and the paragon they promoted was the traditional European city: history's gift to all lovers of walking. The Kriers had shown how the traditional city, with its proportions and grid patterns, is an object lesson in how to plan new cities while Rossi was showing how the traditional European city could be mined for recurring types,[18] all ready and waiting to be mashed into new compositions.[19]

By the 1980s Rossi was an intellectual hero. His best buildings hadn't yet started rusting. Moreover, his best writings had only just been translated, meaning it was only the best teachers – the ones held in the highest regard – who were referring to him when critiquing student work. His idea that, if properly studied, the traditional European city holds all the answers, lent an intellectual air to a period otherwise spoilt by postmodern pastiche. The invitation pregnant in his work to travel to Italy left such an impression on me personally that I now lead annual study tours there. Having worked as an architectural historian since 2001, you could say I was equally impressed by the historiographical dimensions of his theory and practice. So of course it annoys me that his central idea, that the European city be taken as a sourcebook of sorts, has been reduced

10
Simon Sadler, *The Situationist City* (Cambridge, MA: The MIT Press, 1999).

11
Guy Debord, 'Theory of the Dérive', *Les Lèvres Nues*, No. 9 (1956).

12
Will Self, *Psychogeography. Words by Will Self* (London: Bloomsbury Publishing, 2008).

13
Richard Marshall, 'Josef Lluis Sert's Urban Design Legacy', in: *The Urban Design Reader*, Michael Larice and Elizabeth MacDonald (Ed.) (New York: Routledge, 2012), 111.

14
Kevin Lynch, *The Image of the City* (Cambridge, MA: The MIT Press, 1960).

15
Gordon Cullen, *The Concise Townscape* (Oxford: Elsevier Science & Technology Books, 1961).

16
Jane Jacobs, *The Death and Life of Great American Cities* (New York: Random House, 1961); see also: http://innovationecosystem.pbworks.com/w/file/fetch/63349251/DowntownisforPeople.pdf.

17
Anthony Vidler, 'The Third Typology', *Oppositions*, No. 7 (1976), 1-4.

18
Aldo Rossi, *The Architecture of the City* (Cambridge, MA: The MIT Press, 1984).

19
My précis of Rossi's method is a drawn from Broadbent's very accessible summary of Rossi's method. See: Geoffrey Broadbent, *Emerging Concepts in Urban Design* (London: Chapman and Hall, 1996).

to a dogma by hipsters. Ours is a time when every yarn-bombing, glib speaker with their own photo of Piazza Navona can call themselves an 'urbanist'. No wonder trained architects are trying to see good in dumps like Dubai; they have to set themselves apart in some way. The field we studied under professors has been taken over by discount-airline, grand tourists. They wouldn't know Aldo from Valentino.

## Shortcomings of the Traditional City as a Paragon for Environmental Design

On the one hand, it is great that a paragon exists to rival the machine. It is just a shame that the pre-twentieth-century European city does not actually hold all the answers. Take the problem of density. The kinds of densities you find in the centres of Paris or Barcelona are high; high enough that if those cities' streets were cleared of machines cyclists could connect quickly with millions of people. The problem in these old cities is those densities are achieved with simplistic building types designed with little thought to sunlight, ventilation, outlooks and visual and acoustic privacy. Another turn off is the reliance on stairs, something that can't simply be solved by retrofitting new lifts. The typical walk-up in a pre-twentieth-century district has too few apartments to split the cost of a lift and its maintenance – unless the residents are all on high incomes. Without lifts, people go on struggling with babies, strollers and groceries on stairs, and are left parking bikes at the ground level.

Another shortcoming of traditional European cities is that none of them in the 6-million-plus category (and we have to include conurbations to find more than one, London) have average trip times of around half an hour like Dallas-Fort Worth, an exemplary car-centric city and model for the developing world. We are not satisfying the needs of rapidly urbanizing nations, or our own requirements of them, if all we have are twee lessons from Venice or Copenhagen.

A like match in Europe for Dallas-Fort Worth would be the conurbation of the Randstad, comprising Amsterdam, Rotterdam, The Hague and Utrecht. The Randstad and Dallas-Fort Worth cover similar-sized regions and have similar-sized populations. Sadly, Dallas-Fort Worth with its reliance on cars, oil, war and the rest, provides far greater freedom of movement. Connecting with the 6-millionth farthest Texan in Dallas-Fort Worth is a matter of pointing your car in their direction and putting your foot to the floor. Connecting with the 6-millionth farthest Dutchman in the Randstad requires a bit of luck with the high-speed train timetable and the knowhow to use bikes, trams, buses or local trains to finish the journey. One might choose to drive, this is true, but with the motorway network having a fraction of the capacity of networks in Texas, being stuck in a jam is more likely.

If we put aside conurbations and just look at individual cities, there is really only one in the E.U. that might have some lessons for city officials elsewhere who are bracing for millions arriving in new cities at once. That is London, a city with all the paradigmatic building types and perimeter block formations that Rossi and the classical urbanists would have us all copy, and that reached this magical size of 6 million (albeit an arbitrary benchmark for scale) a few decades before the twentieth century and the invention of cars.

One of two things might make it of interest as a model for future large cities. First, it might have fast connections – but it certainly doesn't have those. Train trips from outer boroughs to the centre take over an hour, and that's before you add the walk to the station and the time you spend waiting. Britain's Trades Union Congress (TUC) estimates average commute times of 37.8 minutes each way.[20] Second, it might be small enough for us to be talking about banning all cars and letting cyclists ride from the perimeter to the centre in reasonable time. Unfortunately, the nineteenth-century expansion of the rail network allowed London to balloon to around 1,500 square kilometres. A mother living halfway from the centre, say in Kingston upon Thames, would take over an hour to reach the centre with a baby asleep in her box bike. If riding from Hillingdon, they would more likely give up and turn back. London is insufficiently dense for bike transport to work without motors somewhere in the mix.

## The Elegant Device

The point about paragons may be belaboured, but it isn't arcane. It is actually quite natural that architectural or urban design acts refer back to paragons of one sort or another. Any of us could catch ourselves likening a city to a body, for example by saying its football stadium (or maybe its church) is the heart, that its city hall or university is the brains, and that its neighbourhoods or industrial districts are the hands. The only difference between saying that now and saying it during the Italian Renaissance is that a fifteenth-century Florentine audience would have been super impressed.

The same would be true if ever you caught yourself saying that architecture or city planning should refer to nothing outside its own intrinsic nature, a nature that is plain to the eye at archaeological sites, but which is disguised by layers of artifice in newer buildings. These days you might get a few nods, but in the eighteenth century you would have been in for a standing ovation from grand tourists just back from Greece whose other predilections included Newtonian physics.

The problem we have right now is there are two rival paragons, the machine and the kind of naturally-grown city you find mostly in Europe. A Europhile whose vision for a city that has been inspired by the time honoured scale of alleyways and piazzas is not likely to find support from all those whose hearts are for self-driving or flying cars, while the technophile who imagines a city designed to make the best use of robots and phone apps will find little support from those who cannot see the point while Rome is still standing, supposedly telling us everything we need to know about urban design.

The proposals in this book are unlikely to find support from either camp. Europhiles will be prone to view proposals for double-helical mega blocks or fields of moguls with pedestrian bridges linking their crests as aberrations. They would maintain that after thousands of years of city

20
TUC, 'Commute Times Add Up to Five Extra Weeks Work a Year' (11 November 2011). Available online: https://www.tuc.org.uk/workplace-issues/working-time-holidays/work-life-balance/04-homeworkers/commute-times-add-five-extra, accessed 31 March 2015.

21
Michael Carmona
and Patrick Camiller,
*Haussmann: His Life and
Times and the Making of
Modern Paris* (Paris: Ivan
R. Dee, 2002).

22
Esther da Costa Meyer,
*The Work of Antonio
Sant'Elia: Retreat into the
Future* (New Haven: Yale
University Press, 1995).

23
Marie Kondo, *The
Life-Changing Magic of
Tidying Up: The Japanese
Art of Decluttering and
Organizing* (New York: Ten
Speed Press, 2014).

building in Europe, forms such as these have not even occurred as mutations. As for believers in a technological future, most would see these suggestions as jokes. Surely any new urban-development models should be optimizing conditions for the latest technology, not an invention that has basically not changed since 1890.

The answer to that is that bicycle's endurance for a century and a quarter makes it one invention that has earned the right to have cities and buildings designed with it as their paragon. The urban fabric has been sliced with streets for pedestrians, horse-drawn carriages, gondolas and Napoleon's troops.[21] It has been stretched to impossibly low densities and serviced with ribbons of asphalt for cars. Why not massage cities to fit the dynamics of cycling? You might have read to the end of this book because you're a cycling enthusiast. Politically, cycling enthusiasts don't have the numbers influence anyone. What we need is a paragon like the bicycle, but not so specific, that appeals to non-cycling enthusiasts from both the Europhile and technophile camps.

Such a paragon is already there in the history of modernist architecture. Not all modernists took after the futurists, taking the feeling of sublime mountains and projecting that feeling upon machines.[22] If we only look at its most famous figures of the mid 1920s – Walter Gropius in Germany, Le Corbusier in France, Buckminster Fuller in the U.S. – then yes, the machine age does seem homogenous. Architects were designing buildings that could only be reached by machines and that celebrated their arrival like kings.

However, the situation was different for Russian constructivists. In their newly industrializing cities there weren't so many wealthy bohemians with their own private cars. In fact, half the nation was close to starvation. Machines didn't speak to Russian constructivist architects about speeding or flying, but about rebuilding society and maybe surviving. A series of drawings of machines by Yakov Chernikhov show how the emphasis was on the logic of engineering, not the speed thrills one finds in futurist art. We're looking at an image of a bayonet fitting – a simple 'turn-to-lock' mechanism. Regardless of whether you live for the day when cars will all fly, or when we all live upstairs from cafes, it is likely you can appreciate such an elegant device. I certainly can. If required to pack my life into a few cases to go on a plane, it wouldn't grieve me to say goodbye to my white goods. What I would want to pack are one or two hand tools, my La Pavoni manual espresso machine, my acoustic guitar, a few of my favourite kitchen utensils and of course one or two of my most precious bikes. The rest, in the words of Marie Kondo, I could happily kiss goodbye to.[23]

Or think of it this way, how you are more likely to judge the quality of a house by the quality of its simple devices, like the taps or door hardware. When selecting electric garage openers or air-conditioning units we tend to go for the cheapest – no point investing a fortune in technology that is likely to be superseded – but when selecting simple devices, we tend to go for the best.

The traditional European city is a simple device, but one that humanity has outgrown. It doesn't take account of some simple devices that came along later, like the bike or the wheelchair. It is blind too to the benefits of living in a city of millions, not thousands, and the access to markets that large cities give us – or would give us, if we had some way of ensuring quick transport connections.

The building types and new urban development patterns presented in this book are simple devices. We have tried to imagine a city of 6 million people enjoying faster transport connections across the whole city than anyone enjoys in a car or train city. Rather than powered machines like lifts, air-conditioners, rail carriages or cars, we have started on a search for elegant spatial arrangements that revolve around simple devices, like bikes.

Our longer journey begins with our finding that the more we increase permeability at the ground level (think pilotis, fine grids and the likes) and density (think Manhattan), while limiting the encumbrance to cycling posed by large machines (trucks, cars, etcetera), the more elegant a city is likely to be as a human connection device.

How can we bring about such a change? By first understanding that it is we who make space. That might seem like an odd thing to say until you consider that in everyday life space is not where the stars are. Neither is it something we go around measuring on the x-, y- and z-axes. Space is what people navigate as they move through their cities. If they have found their way to the supermarket they are occupying space that was created by road engineers. If they have found their way home they're in a space that traffic engineers unlocked for new houses with new or newly widened main roads. If they are driving their children to school they are navigating their way to space that traffic engineers said could be accessed by slip lanes. If they find themselves at work in an industrial park they are likewise in space chosen according to the logic of traffic engineering.

We're told all this must be as it is because people like cars, and because cars would stop one another from moving if the production of space didn't revolve around frictionless roadways. It doesn't matter that the profession designing those roadways has been inspired by the design of big sewers – meaning people are being treated like faeces. We're still too impressed by their triumphs. Economic juggernaut cities like Dallas-Fort Worth and Los Angeles became what they are thanks to incredible roads. It doesn't matter that there is no money now to maintain them. It doesn't matter that economic conditions don't favour them being replicated, properly, elsewhere in the world. The money will come from their building, or somewhere, we hope.

But in the end we must hope that the developing world never succeeds the way we have with highways and cars. We're already on track for severe global warming. If the world's 5 billion poor manage to build highways and buy cars, there will be no hope at all. What we really need is for the world's richest (now driving) and poorest (just walking) to meet in the middle (all cycling).

4.bp.blogspot.com, 230
Leon Battista Alberti, 229
Andthenimovedto.com, 207
Hakim Ahmet, 162
Amsterdam.nl, 66
Archdaily.com, 208, 211
Architizer.com, 208
Archspace.com, 179
Autospeed.com, 161
Ashton Raggat McDougal, 162
Astro.rug.nl, 66
Iwan Baan, 162
Peter Baab, 183
Behance.net, 208
Norman Bel Geddes, 20, 100, 106
Alfred Beach, 62
BIG, 93, 97, 100, 162, 179, 195
Britishpathe.com, 58
Butchersandbicycles.com, 90
Byron, 61
Italo Calvino, 106
Iakov Chernikhov, 230
Charles Chua, 162
CEBRA and GLIFBERG+LYKKE,
    162
Choice.com.au, 37
Mikael Colville-Andersen, 8, 12, 15,
    16, 32, 70, 86, 111, 112, 122, 134,
    144, 193, 200
Corbis, 220
J. H. Crawford, 127
Cyclingchristchurch.co.nz, 167
Dailytonic.com, 208
Francesco de Gergio, 90, 229
Bryan De Grineau, 50
Leonardo da Vinci, 229
Dezeen.com, 95, 180, 211
Charlie Dumais, 190
Bill Dunster, 165
Martin Ebert, 47, 124
Economist.com, 183
Ecowatch.com, 190
Harriet Elliot, 118, 119, 120, 137, 139,
    176, 184, 190
Epomm.eu, 40, 66
Exolo.us, 208
M.C. Escher, 154
Carl Fieger, 214
Fietsberaad.nl, 66
Fingolas, 183
fondazionealdorossi.org, 230
Buckminster Fuller, 103
Steven Fleming, 20, 23, 24, 54,
    58, 66, 78, 121, 127, 131, 143, 152,
    165, 166, 176, 180, 207, 238
Jordi Gali, 165

Scott Gelson, 204
Gensler architecture, 190
Bob Gomel, 21
Google Earth, 22, 58
Gittings, 190
Tom Hatton, 140, 141, 142, 184
Helmoftherepublican.com, 183
Ludwig Hilberseimer, 157
James Ho, 162
David Holoka, 131
Ebeneza Howard, 61, 127
ipv Delft, 193
itdp.org, 173
itu.dk, 95
Jamie Jimenez, 208
Rob Jetson, 169
Jensen-Architects.com, 211
Jiakan Architects, 179
Brian Jones, 190
Louis I. Kahn Collection, 97
Leon Krier, 230
KGP Design Studios, 220
Marc-Antoine Laugier, 229
Le Corbusier, 93, 158, 229
Claud Nicolas Ledoux, 95, 103
llnl.gov, 37
LSECities.net, 187
Rene Magritte, 109
Rob Maver, 78, 79, 80, 81, 82, 166
Moronocity.com, 40
Charlotte Morton, 10, 19, 24, 25,
    26, 27, 28, 29, 30, 31, 103, 152,
    154, 157, 158, 162, 176, 207
NASA, 50
Next Architects, 194
nj.com, 50
Oddculture.com, 128
Officelovin.com, 207
Dominique Perrault, 93, 220
pinkbike.com, 40
Alex Proimos, 138
RAAD Studio, 190
Reuters/China Daily, 61
Stuart Robinson, 162
Aldo Rossi, 230
Matt Samson, 162
Abdel Soudan, 76, 77, 83, 84, 85,
    154, 158, 173
straitstimes.com, 166
TED.com, 37
Ben Thorp, 91, 115, 116, 117, 187
UN Studio, 211
untappedcities.com, 163
villa-poissy.fr, 54
vhi.com, 128
want.nl, 187

Mark Wagenbuur, 152
Nathan Wheatley, 204
Wikipedia commons, 22, 47, 62,
    93, 97, 103, 109, 128, 148, 157,
    173, 187, 207, 229
Johann Winckelmann, 229
Zandrikuun, 53

The book *Velotopia* is published in association with Cycle Space Amsterdam

www.cyclespace.nl

**Special thanks**
The research by design method gets better with every additional designer and this project had almost two hundred—more if you count interlocutors who criticized early design explorations at public lectures. Over a hundred participants in my "cycle space" design studios, mainly at the University of Tasmania, but also in workshops held at the Queensland Museum and the National Museum of Australia, fed design investigations with their ideas; my thanks go to them all and also Stephen Loo, Daniel Oakman and Angelina Russo for giving me the opportunity to lead those studios. Rafael Upcroft, Ben Thorp, Charlotte Morton, Harriet Elliot, Amy Pedder, Rob Maver and Abdel Soudan gave up their Summers to help push the design process further again. It was Ng Khai Jie, with her tutor Geoff Clark, who first thought of stacking "slip blocks".

I'm grateful to everyone who commented on work in progress, whether on my blog cycle-space. com or websites like City Lab and Arch Daily. Thank you Ben Thorp, Christiaan Zandstra, Detlef Prince and Sven Prince for feedback on drafts. Ben Thorp and Wendy Roberts provided research assistance.

The following people will know how I've made use of knowledge I have gained from my associations with them: Michael Chapman, Anne Lusk, Lee Roberts, Rafael Upcroft, Ceridwen Owen, Daniel Oakman, Angelina Russo, Monica Zarafu and Martin Ebert.

For knowledge from their local contexts I need to thank Francis Chu, David Holowka, Rebecca Short, David Borella, Mark Wagenbuur, Pascal van den Noort and my associates in Amsterdam, Lee Feldman, Roos Stallinga, Maud de Vries, Maarten Woolthuis, Nick Feeney and Floortje Vermeer.

Knowing the following people believed in this work was all the encouragement I needed to persevere: Eelco van Welie, Marcel Witvoet, Rob Cooper and my beloved car-free family Kerry, Aquinas and Atlas Fleming.

Special thanks to Mikael Colville-Andersen for generously providing so many of his photos, and to the people of Copenhagen for being so sophisticated riding their bikes.

Steven Fleming, 2017

**Illustration credits**
Key producers of images for this book have been Mikael Colville-Andersen, Ben Thorp, Rob Maver, Abdel Soudan, Harriet Elliot, Charlotte Morton, Rafael Upcroft, Sadia Abedin, Martin Ebert, Brian Jones, Tom Hatton, Aquinas Fleming, David Holowka, Amir Taheri, Stuart Robinson, Chau Hin Lim Charles, James Ho, Hakim Ahmat and Nathan Wheatley.

**Texts**
Steven Fleming

**Copy editing**
Mehgan Bakhuizen

**Design**
75B

**Lithography and printing**
NPN Drukkers

**Publisher**
Marcel Witvoet,
nai010 publishers

nai010 publishers is an internationally orientated publisher specialized in developing, producing and distributing books in the fields of architecture, urbanism, art and design. www.nai010.com

nai010 books are available internationally at selected bookstores and from the following distribution partners:
North, Central and South America - Artbook | D.A.P., New York, USA, dap@dapinc.com
Rest of the world - Idea Books, Amsterdam, the Netherlands, idea@ideabooks.nl
For general questions, please contact nai010 publishers directly at sales@nai010.com or visit our website www.nai010.com for further information.

Printed and bound in the Netherlands
ISBN 978-94-6208-352-3

Also available as e-book (pdf)
*Velotopia* (pdf)
ISBN 978-94-6208-368-4